A Taste for Paprika

A TASTE for PAPRIKA

❦

LAURA ELISE TAYLOR

Enjoy!
Laura

Shoreline

Copyright, Laura Elise Taylor, 2004

Cover photo: Laura Elise Taylor
Cover design: Kathe Gray
Cover consultant: Scott Mooney
Interior design: Kathe Gray
Editor: Megan Morrissey

Printed in Canada by AGMV Marquis

Published by Shoreline, 23 Ste-Anne
Ste-Anne-de-Bellevue, Quebec, Canada H9X 1L1
Phone/Fax 514-457-5733
shoreline@sympatico.ca   www.shorelinepress.ca

Epigraph from "Rezeptfrei" in *Wenn's doch nur so einfach wär,*
reprinted by permission of the author.
English translation by Laura Elise Taylor

Dépôt legal: National Library of Canada
Et la Bibliothèque nationale du Québec

National Library of Canada Cataloguing in Publication

Taylor, Laura Elise, 1975-
A Taste for Paprika / Laura Elise Taylor

Originally presented as the author's thesis
(M.A.–University of Alberta, 2000)
ISBN 1-896754-36-8

I. Title.

PS8589.A898T38 2004   C813'.6   C2004-903981-4

Für Oma

And for my mother—
so far we've come

*Rezepte für das Leben
kann ich nicht geben.*

*Woher
soll ich wissen,
welche Zutaten
deinen Kuchen
gelingen lassen?*

Recipes for life
I cannot give.

How
can I know
which ingredients
will make
your cake rise?

KRISTIANE ALLERT-WYBRANIETZ

Descendants of Barbara Shanta

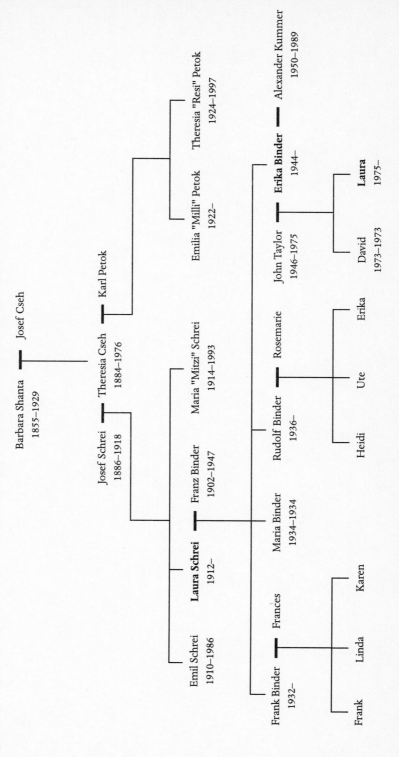

ONE

Ingredients

A N AUTUMN WITHOUT *Zwetschgenknödel* is a sad, wasted season. Only occasionally can I find the proper plums—not too big, not too hard—but when I do, and the pink plum-blood bleeds into the pale potato dough, the taste is heaven.

The recipe for *Zwetschgenknödel*—plum dumplings—is one my Oma carried in her memory from *da Hoam* when she immigrated to Canada with her daughter, my mother, on April first, 1958. Even after forty years, "home" for Oma—Laura Binder, née Schrei—is still Jakobshof, the tiny German-speaking hamlet perched on the border between Austria and Hungary where she was born in 1912.

When Oma was a girl, Jakobshof was a place where children ran barefoot in the fields from Easter until the first snow. A place where the rhythm of life was dictated by planting and harvest, by potato blossoms and wine making. A place where women sat together shelling pumpkin seeds on winter evenings, speculating about coming dances, gossiping about shady pregnancies, sharing secrets of men and yeast. A place where doors were never locked.

Until the war. There comes a point in every story when Oma's face darkens. *"Und dann sind die Russen gekommen,"* she says. And then the Russians came. When the Eastern Front swept through Jakobshof in 1944, Oma was alone with her three children. Frank was twelve, Rudi ten, and Erika, my mother, an infant. My Opa, Franz Binder, had been forced to enlist, and hadn't been heard from in months. "You can't imagine all we went through," Oma says, before launching into stories some say a child shouldn't hear.

Things didn't improve for the villagers after the war ended. For centuries, the border had swished back and forth like a horse's tail.

And over those centuries, the people who called this piece of land home danced and worked and died without taking much interest in the machinations of empires or nation-states. "We were stupid," Oma always says, "but we were happy."

After the war, the location of the border became the most crucial element in their world. At the Potsdam Conference, the victors ruled that all ethnic Germans from the newly-defined neighbouring states be returned to the German "homeland." These people — called *Flüchtlinge*, refugees, *Volksdeutsche*, DPs — from Czechoslovakia, Poland, Yugoslavia and Hungary, numbered over fifteen million. There are estimates that over two million died during or as a result of this forced mass relocation.

In 1946, the Hungarian government used the Potsdam ruling to deport all German-speakers, ethnic German or otherwise. Whole villages, including Jakobshof, whose inhabitants still held Austrian passports from before the establishment of the 1920 border with Hungary, were deported to a Germany too ruined by war not to resent additional mouths to feed. On any map published after 1946 you will not find Jakobshof, only Jakabhaza. The new Hungarian communist government did its best to erase all evidence that this region was ever anything but Hungarian.

After eleven years of feeling unwelcome in Germany, Oma was more than happy to leave. Only her second son, Rudi, and his wife stayed in the southern German town of Pleidelsheim; everyone else who mattered was either dead or missing or already in North America.

Oma's oldest son, Frank, had left Pleidelsheim eight years before, and scraped together enough money to pay for his mother and younger sister to join him and his growing family in Ontario.

WHEN THE AIRPLANE BEGAN ITS DESCENT into Toronto, my mother, a quiet, blond thirteen-year-old, looked out over the chaotic assortment of roofs — green, black, even turquoise. I imagine her sitting as far forward as she can to get a better view, twisting the open edge of her cardigan until the zipper left dark purple tracks across her palm. No neat, red-clay shingles in sight. Nobody who spoke her language, no friends, nobody. She looked over at Oma, who was sitting with her rough hands folded in her lap, eyes forward, probably worrying about food. They didn't speak. I see my mother sink into her seat, thinking, How can you do this to me?

This, at least, is how I picture it. Imagine, for a moment, living your whole life, save six delicious years, with your mother.

HOME FOR ME IS THE HOUSE in Port Credit, Ontario, where I grew up. My mother and father, Erika and John, bought the Cape Cod-style fixer-upper in 1974. When, a few months later, the old man for whom Oma had been housekeeper died, she moved in with my parents. My father, with his sensual eyes and handsome dark hair, spent the following year working on the house with a passion. Nineteen seventy-five was the year of my birth, the year of my father's death. I was born into a line of women who lose the men they have loved. But I try not to believe in curses.

In 1993, Oma, my mother and I went to Budapest to visit Oma's sisters. On the way back to Austria we drove through Jakobshof. The cart-track that once divided the village's two rows of houses had become a major highway, and the traffic of heavy trucks was constant. Shortly before we reached the village, it started to pour. Sheets of water fell faster than the windshield wipers could clear them. My mother managed to pull over and let the trucks blast past us. I wiped a circle in the fogged window and looked out for the first time at *da Hoam*. Only it wasn't.

"There's the house I was born in," Oma said, pointing to a dilapidated building. "And there's the schoolhouse. And the *Gasthaus*. And the cemetery. So, that's it," she said, "now we can go."

I was glad we couldn't linger. This drab, grey place was no match for the world Oma had cooked up for me. When I was a child, the Jakobshof she created, linked with garlic cloves and hot paprika, was a more exciting, vivid place than the world I knew. What's the point, I thought then, in going back?

MY MOTHER LOVES TO EAT, can eat twice as much as I can and stays twice as thin. But she is not a natural cook. My stepfather, Alexander, was a good cook. I remember he had a sweet tooth comparable to mine, and that he hated raisins. He said they just got bigger and bigger in his mouth until he couldn't swallow. Actually, both of my mother's husbands liked to work with food. Maybe that is why, when Oma and I join forces in the kitchen, my mother steers clear of us. Oma works from memory. This is something my mother avoids whenever she can.

I was raised on the foods from *da Hoam*, and on its stories. In our family's bright, red-and-white suburban kitchen, Oma taught me to measure ingredients in my cupped hands, to roll the names of far-away people and places on my tongue in Austrian-German.

Now, thousands of kilometers from our house in Port Credit and the kitchen in which I spent so much of my childhood, I have periodic cravings for the sound of Oma's voice. When I am floundering around in my own kitchen, I pray that my hands will remember the measurements, that my fingers will still know the right consistency of the dough. And when my lips are stained with the sour-sweet plum juice of the *Zwetschgenknödel*, I can still find my way back to the world Oma conjured over steaming soup pots and sizzling *Schnitzel*.

This is not the whole story. Ask my mother her opinion of what follows and she will tell you, "Well, that's one perspective. I see things differently." Ask her to elaborate, and she will shake her lovely, youthful head, saying, "Don't ask."

Fair enough. We each have our own recipes for history, our own ways of blending the ingredients of memory into a palatable tale. What follows are my Oma's stories, as I have heard them since before I could talk. And my mother's story, as best I can guess it. Ultimately, though, this recipe is mine.

TWO

Home

Mohnstrudel

"*A*ZUCKER BRAUCH'MA," OMA SAYS. I reach with sure hands into the cupboard under the kitchen counter to find the sugar tin. Oma lists the other ingredients we will need for the *Mohnstrudel* and we gather them on the counter. I run my fingers along the familiar contours of the white and red cupboards that are exactly as old as I am. It is good to be back.

"Come, smell," Oma says as she opens the bag of freshly ground poppy seeds, the *Mohn* for the *Strudel*. She has bought the seeds at Kensington Market in Toronto. They are surprisingly moist, and smell of earth. Oma holds the bag to her nose and breathes deeply.

"The fields *da Hoam*," she says, "they were always full of flowers, every colour you can imagine. Blue cornflowers and yellow Raps, purple lilacs that had this sweet, sweet smell in the spring. And *Mohn*, poppies there were, red and orange and yellow. But mostly red. Not the big ugly ones you see here, no." She shakes her head. "Ours were small, with petals like fine paper. They grew wild on the edges of the *Feldwege*, the paths where the hay wagons and ploughs drove. In the evenings when the wind was still, from high up on the hay wagon, they looked like tiny drops of paint, or blood maybe, so bright they were. *Ja*. Fields that beautiful I have never seen since, over here."

I hold the *Mohn* to my nose and breathe deeply.

"I've missed you, Oma."

"*Ja*," she replies, and hugs me. Her fine, grey-brown hair barely reaches my chin now, but her embrace is fierce as ever. When I was little I believed that people died by shrinking away until they disappeared.

Oma empties a packet of yeast into a cup of warm water and I feed it a spoonful of sugar.

"Are you still afraid of *Hefe?*" Oma asks as the cup fills with coffee-coloured froth. She inches it across the counter toward me and I laugh.

"Oma, did you eat a lot of *Mohn* back in Hungary?"

"Oh, *ja*. Lots of people had *Mohn* growing in their gardens. We used it for baking, or with sugar over egg-noodles. Oh, *ja*, it was good.

"One day when it was ripe, my friend Rosa and I, we had this craving for fresh poppy seeds. We were young, maybe eight years old. So we snuck into *der* Jost's garden when he was away, and we stole all the *Mohn* he had growing there, picked it all and wrapped it in our aprons. And then we ran as fast as we could out through the fields to the forest. We hid in the forest way off the path and cracked open the pods and ate and ate. So good it tasted, crunching those fresh seeds. We ate and ate like little goats who don't know when to stop." Oma shakes her head and chuckles.

"And then Rosa looked at me and said, 'I don't feel too good.' Right when she said that I tried to get up, but I couldn't. All of a sudden I was so dizzy, so dizzy. Rosa was leaning over a log, retching. We were so sick."

"Oma, are you sure people grew poppies only for baking?" I ask.

"*Ha,* it is only in the seed pod, the top part that is dangerous. The seeds are all right," she says.

"So you did know."

"Oh, *ja*," she says dismissively. "And when we finally could walk again, we tried to sneak home, but my mother was waiting for us in the kitchen. She was so mad. 'Did you steal *der* Jost's *Mohn?*' she asked us. We shook our heads, but she knew it was us, with our stained aprons and sick faces. She put her hand on my forehead and sighed. *Der* Jost had reported the theft to the police, and she would have to pay him for all we stole. 'Go to bed, both of you,' my mam said. She could tell that we had already punished ourselves."

"Oh, come on, Oma. Surely this Jost wasn't using his *Mohn* for baking, if he bothered to report a bunch of missing flowers to the police."

"*Ha,* he was like that." She shrugs. "But fresh *Mohn* you will have to try, Laura. It's so good."

We mix the ingredients together in silence. Just as Oma cuts a large slab of butter to add, I hear my mother coming downstairs. She swoops into the room, looking elegant even in her gardening clothes—tapered jeans, an orange sweatshirt and grass-stained shoes. Her fine, frosted blond hair is teased back from striking, chiselled features. At the sight of the block of yellow fat on the counter, her steel blue eyes narrow in disapproval.

"Laura, don't let her use so much butter this time," she scolds. "It's not necessary."

Since when are you the expert, I think, but say nothing. Oma sighs a soul-rattling sigh. They exchange a hard glance.

My mother turns back to me. "And if you two are really planning to drive to Frank's today, shouldn't you be packing instead of fiddling around in the flour? This is no time for stories. It'll take you three hours to drive up there, and it gets dark early, remember."

"Yes, Mother," I say. She knows my Onkel Frank asked for the *Strudel.* She knows Oma asked me to help her bake it. It was even her idea that I drive Oma to my uncle's for this weekend visit. I continue to stir in the flour.

The jaw beneath my mother's high, lovely cheekbones tenses. "Fine, do what you want," she calls to us as she climbs back upstairs, "but don't blame me if you drive off a cliff in the dark."

When we are alone again, Oma goes straight for the butter and adds another chunk. I do nothing. She looks at me and starts to laugh, low and rolling, but weary.

Mom, I haven't been in this house twenty-four hours yet and you are already annoyed with me. You complain that I don't come home often enough, but I'm not sure it's a good idea that I do. I've fallen out of the rhythm of your life, I'm a disruption now. I've forgotten how to be silent, how to avoid disturbing the dust that has settled on your memories.

This is not the time for stories, you always say. Is it because there is too much going on, too much energy required for ordinary living to risk the storm that a look into the past might stir up inside you? Everyone is amazed at how well you hold it together after all you have been though. Today, you say, today life is good. Be thankful. And I am, I am. But there is so much I want to know, so much I need your help to understand.

I've lived away from home for five years. Alexander's been dead for ten. The dust is thick.

WHEN I POUR THE YEAST into the mixing bowl, it fizzes and flows like lava in the flour.

Oma watches me knead the ingredients into a sticky dough. With a rhythmic push and pull I send it around the bowl until it is even and soft.

"Sichst's, gut kannst es schon, look how well you do it," she says, nodding with approval.

"I hope so, Oma. You taught me how."

I cover the dough with a cloth and set it in the warm oven to rise. "It's sleeping," Oma used to tell me. "We must be quiet so the yeast can dream and grow big."

"You know where I made my first Mohnstrudel? At the Kastelln," Oma says.

"A castle?" I ask.

"Ja, sort of. The Kastelln was just past the village, on the same road. Grafs, nobles from Budapest lived there. The old countess was a widow, and had three children, two daughters and a son. It was so beautiful, so big. It's too bad they tore it down after the war. It was three storeys, and each of the young countesses had a room and each had her own servants. Two cooks they had, two washerwomen, teachers for the children, a chauffeur for their car, and beautiful carriage horses, six or seven. And out in the woods was a little house where they generated electricity for the lights and everything. Our village had never seen electricity. Some people were suspicious.

"In the summers I worked at the Kastelln, in the kitchen all day. That was when I was nine, ten years old. We were two helpers in the kitchen, me and Rosa. In the morning when the Gräfin came into the kitchen to order the meals for the day we had to curtsy and greet her, but most of the time we ran away when she came, and hid behind the cupboards until she was done."

"Was she mean?"

"Oh, no, she talked with us servants as she talked with everyone. But we were shy.

"The girls…Edeka and—what was her name? They were so elegant in their long dresses, and so clever. There was a piano, and I would peek through the doors to watch them playing and singing. I'd never heard such music. I listened and watched until the cook caught me and pulled me back to the kitchen. My friend Rosa and I, we practiced walking like the countesses, all elegant, *nit*, but when they wanted to talk with us, we were too shy to speak. Their *Deutsch* was so proper, and we spoke such a mish-mash."

Do you remember, Mom, when you used to take me for rambles on that old estate in the country? We would walk out past the crumbling buildings and abandoned gardens, pretending we owned them. You would take my hand and we would wade through fields so high with wild grasses and milkweed that if we crouched low no one could find us. I can still see the wind playing in those fields, how it would send ripples through the grasses like waves in water.

You told me lots of stories then. Stories about Germany, and growing up. About sneaking into the fields just past the barracks, taking big steps so the farmer wouldn't catch you trampling his hay. About lying concealed in those fields with your friends Waltraud and Wiltraud on empty summer afternoons, finding heroes in the clouds. About the daisy tiaras you wove and the handsome Grafs you married, Grafs who sometimes had the faces of boys in the next grade at school. Yes, you said, it seems to me we spent a lot of time dreaming. Of marriage, mostly. Our world was so small. What else was there to dream of?

I DUMP THE BLOATED DOUGH onto the table and roll it out. With a glance at the stairs, Oma moistens it generously with melted shortening.

"So it sticks," she explains. We take handfuls of poppy and sugar and sprinkle the dough until it is covered in a thick, black coat. Standing side by side, our arms touching, we roll up the strudel with careful fingers until it is a long, pale-gold log. Oma applies more shortening as a glaze for the top.

"Our favourite work at the *Kastelln* was on the day before big parties," Oma says. "We made *Strudel*—apple and poppy-seed, meringues and little cream tarts. But the best was when we made ice cream. That was my job, mine and Rosa's. We took turns churning this big vat filled with the cream and sugar and vanilla and everything."

"They had ice?"

"*Alles, alles* they had. Ice in summer, a motorcar, electric light. No one else had any of these things. We were poor, *nit*, poor and stupid.

"And when the ice cream was done, we cleaned the edges of the vat with our fingers and licked and licked, it was so good."

Mom, you used to tell me about the milk kitchen in town, of the sweet, peculiar smell that would greet you every morning when you lined up for the daily ration. Of how you would linger after the pails were filled, clusters of boys and girls gossiping and making eyes at each other until doors along the street would open and your mothers called you home.

You told me about the black and white storks and their nest on the bell tower of the church. Of your first job, babysitting in the shadow of the tower and praying that the storks wouldn't crow and wake the sleeping child. Of wondering whether the parents would count their silverware after you left.

Being friends with local children like Waltraud and Wiltraud was tough sometimes, wasn't it? Waltraud's mother was nice enough, but she would let a Flüchtlingskind, a refugee like you, only as far as the front steps, never into the house. You only saw the inside of Wiltraud's home when you went with Oma on cleaning jobs, and remember being deathly afraid of the telephone, tiptoeing around for fear it would ring. And you saw your first full bathroom there, with a tub and a flush toilet. So how did you wash when you lived in the old barracks, I asked when you told me this story. We spot-washed, you said, a bit here a bit there, like the queen.

THE OVEN DOOR CREAKS as Oma opens it. I slide our *Strudel* into the heat and check the clock. I love the measured, unrushable pace of baking, the delicious bits of time spent in anticipation. Oma and I settle in at the table.

"And every day when I worked at the *Kastelln*," she says, "I had to go for drinking water because their well was not good. To Binder's house I went, because it was closest. And every day *der* Franz would greet me and fill my pails."

"My Opa?" I ask.

"*Ja.* That was him. I never thought I would marry him, never. He was a grown man, almost twenty, *nit*, and running the biggest farm around, and I was still a girl.

"But we all grew up faster then. The *Gräfin's* son, *der* Michael he was called, he was a big, handsome *Kerl* who flirted with everyone, even with us. For a while I dreamed he would marry me and then I would have long dresses and eat ice cream every day. So stupid!

"It came out that he went every day with his fancy horse to St. Gotthard, to the whorehouse there. He said it himself. And after a time, Michael made so many debts that they had to sell and move back to Budapest.

"I didn't eat ice cream again after that until we came to Canada."

Mom, do you remember poking around the coach house at the old estate and finding that horseshoe with nails still in it? Hang it over the door, points up, you said, to catch the luck.

We searched the overgrown pathways for the weeds with the tiny heart-shaped leaves winding up their stems, weeds that tell fortunes more accurately than daisies. Instead of he loves me, he loves me not, there are six possibilities as you pluck the hearts from the stem:

Er liebt mich von Herzen	*He loves me from the heart*
mit Schmertzen	*with pains*
über alle Masen	*over everything*
ganz rasend	*like crazy*
ein wenig	*a little*
oder gar nicht.	*or not at all.*

I can see you hiding alone in the field after Oma has told you of her plans to emigrate. Each weed you pluck tells you that the boy who so boldly catches your eye every morning at the milk kitchen, the one with the dark eyes and gypsy features, loves you like crazy. You are as certain as only a thirteen-year-old can be. And now you are leaving. So you cry, and crush the tiny hearts until your hands are sticky and green.

But then I see you hugging your knees in to your chest and beginning to change your dreams. Beginning to wonder what this Kanada might be like for you.

Mom, if you won't tell me these stories any more, I'm going to tell them for you. For us.

THE AROMA OF BAKING *Mohnstrudel* billows out from the oven until it fills every space in the house, beckoning. I set the finished loaf on a rack to cool just as my mother reappears in the kitchen doorway.

"So, is it done yet?" she asks.

"Has to cool first," I reply, sitting down at the table again. I pull out a chair for her, but she has already drifted to the window. With her hands on the sill, she looks out at the green, moist shade cast by the old oaks and maples in our back garden, and sighs.

"So," Oma continues, "after the *Grafs* left, I went with twelve years to St. Gotthard to work for a family. And at sixteen I went to the textile factory, and with eighteen, in 1930, I was married. And so it went, *nit*. By then, Franz was farming the lands of the *Kastelln*, he had a lot of land. And the factory gave me lots of material, so then I could have my nice dresses. But we worked like dogs, so I had no time to wear them." She chuckles. "And then the war came and we lost everything, anyways."

I cut the loaf through the middle, and set half aside to take north.

"Beautiful!" Oma exclaims when she sees the deep-brown swirl of *Mohn* in the golden bread. I cut her a slice. She beckons to my mother. "Come Erika, sit, eat."

My mother takes a piece but remains standing. The steaming *Strudel* cupped in her hands, she surveys the kitchen, pensive. Her gaze pauses at the fruit bowl overflowing with bananas and kiwis, at the new microwave that Oma refuses to touch. She turns and looks out into the living room, with its pine fireplace and piano in the corner.

"Yes," my mother says. "How far we've come."

There is a silence. I motion again to the chair. She shakes her head as if to clear it and looks at her watch.

"All right, you two," she says briskly, "it's getting late. Frank will be worried."

As we pack up our creation in tin foil and dishcloths, it occurs to me that I used to hate *Mohnstrudel*. It took me years and lots of sugar to acquire a taste for it. Now that I live far away I find myself craving the bitter-sweet poppy seeds. But I can still handle only one slice at a time.

The Judenmarkt

*B*ARRING SICKNESS AND IMPOSSIBLE WEATHER, Oma has not missed one Wednesday afternoon at the bingo club since she joined, sometime in the sixties. Her day off, she calls it. Every Wednesday morning when I was little, Oma would slip out of her house-shift and let me choose a brooch to fasten at the neck of the good dress she would wear for the trip downtown. Then she would tie a blue, gauze-thin head kerchief over the curls she had risen early to unwrap, check her purse for subway tokens, sticky candies and bingo chips, and be off to the train.

For the communities nestled along the north shore of Lake Ontario, "downtown" means Toronto. On a clear day, the skyline of the city is visible from the harbour in Port Credit. Oma once told me that the CN tower was a needle for stitching clouds together, and I believed her.

On this mid-summer day, I have taken the GO-train into Toronto to meet up with Oma after bingo. "She's going to go shopping," my mother said this morning with thinly controlled exasperation, "and she knows she'll be stiff tomorrow if she schleps too much. But I can't tell her anything these days. Why don't you go help her?"

The basement of St. Patrick's Catholic Church on McCaul Street has been the gathering site for the German-speaking congregation for decades now. As I brush past the signboard outside, I notice that there is only one German language service scheduled. Two are in Korean, one in Portuguese. Much has changed in the twenty years since I last came to Bingo with Oma, but as I descend the sagging stairs to the hall, the memories return.

THE CAVERNOUS HALL IS LINED with long rows of wobbly tables. It is 1980, and the little girl I once was perches on a chair, her legs swinging, taking everything in. The caller, a thin man with hair growing out of his ears, squints at each ball in turn and speaks into the reverberating microphone. Oh fifty-tree, he says carefully. Eye neun. Jee twenty-fife.

The little girl surveys the figures around her, hunched in concentration over their cards. She thinks of turtles.

Bingo! someone shouts, waving a hand. Immediate grumbles follow: She won again? How could she win again when I haven't won once? She always wins. Must be fixed. Look, here and here, I needed only one more. Only one more! Oh, you shut up already, let's play again.

Each card costs a penny, and almost two hundred and fifty people play, so on a good day Oma might win five dollars in change. She would come home and rattle her penny jar. "I'm rich, I'm rich," she'd say and laugh.

Coffee and buns are served at the break. The girl tucks her legs up and munches a bun, listening to Oma and her friends. Around the table, the singsong of Hungarian-German blends with dialects from Czechoslovakia, Yugoslavia, Poland — every German dialect imaginable, except what is spoken in Germany.

Frau Schnoltzer has brought tomatoes and zucchini from her garden. "I live alone," she says. "For what should I keep so much?" Frau Schnoltzer comes from Oberradling, Oma tells her granddaughter; they were practically neighbours *da Hoam*. "Everyone here has such a story," she says, "someone should write a book."

Her friends Anna and Maria are exchanging recipes for stain removers.

"Those two are from Yugoslavia," says Oma. "During the war, their whole valley packed up and fled the Russian massacres. They fled in big caravans in wagons pulled by horses or oxen, like you see on the television. What's that show? Like on *Little House on the Prairie. Ja*, they fled up the main road north, the very road I lived on, *nit*. And now we are friends. All these years."

The women in Oma's circle lean together, gossiping and laughing. Eyes water as the conversation swings back and forth across the ocean, across the decades. The little girl feels very far from Port Credit. With her eyes closed, she imagines that Lake Ontario has swelled past its shores and that she is on a tiny island with these women who have come from so far. Again she thinks of turtles, carrying their homes on their backs. She understands little of their grown-up conversation, but it does not matter. Everyone smiles, and she knows she belongs.

REACHING THE BOTTOM OF THE STAIRS, I push open the heavy doors of the hall. At first glance the room is empty, but at the far end, a few figures sit hunched. I count eight curly, grey heads spaced along the tables as though holding places for those who can no longer come. Oma looks up and waves me over. I walk past watery eyes, walkers and canes, to sit by her. I know Oma reads the obituaries every day. I know that there have been many funerals. But the obtrusive echo of my footsteps in this empty space makes me feel sick.

Oma is beaming, so pleased that she can show me off. Her friends all smile their welcome and seem to know who I am. I smile back and do not confess that I recognize no one. Someone, I think it is Frau Schnolzer, asks a question in halting English. *Sie kann ja Deutsch,* Oma tells her proudly. Oooohhh, they chorus in surprise, for none of their grandchildren speak German. And in forty years, they have not learned English.

The games are over mercifully soon, and the women shuffle slowly out. At 86, Oma is the youngest.

"It's hardly worth coming anymore," she says when we are outside, "they are all so old."

We are going to Kensington market, a few blocks west. The *Judenmarkt,* Oma calls it.

"THE STORES BACK HOME in St. Gotthard, our shopping town, half of them were owned by *die Juden,*" Oma says as we walk. "*Ja,* the other stores, they thought they were too good for us, *nit,* too good for the farm people. But the Jews, they were good. I always went to the Jews.

One woman, *die* Frau Weiss, Anna, she would always call to me when I was riding by on my bicycle. 'Laura,' she would say, '*komm schau,* I have new *Kopftierchel* for you.' That was the style, you know, these kerchiefs we wore over our hair. And we were always collecting the newest colours. Sometimes with stripes or dots, checkered. And Anna would always keep aside the pretty ones for me. She was a good-looking woman with dark hair, thick curls around her face. I can still see her standing in the doorway, waving those handfuls of kerchiefs at us.

"When I was pregnant the first time, with Frank, I didn't have anything, I didn't know anything, *nit.* So I went to the Weiss store, and Anna took me by the hand, and led me behind the curtain to the storage shelves, and showed me everything I would need. *Die Windeln,* the diapers, you know, everything I would need for a baby, even the christening cushion, she brought me. We made a big pile on the counter. She had a little girl herself, and she gave me some things she was finished with for free. And the other stuff…'Pay me when you can,' she always said. She was so good. Only the Jews would let us pay on credit. Never in those rich Hungarian stores."

Oma tells me that Kensington used to be the Jewish quarter, thirty years ago. Most of the bagel bakeries and kosher delis are long gone, and the void has been filled by cheese shops, vegetable stands, stores selling fresh fish or meat. Aromas of curries and peppers blend with the smells of bread baking and the stench of fish. Signs proclaim the wares and prices in Portuguese, Spanish, Italian, Cantonese. Oma navigates the narrow, crowded streets with a calm assuredness, pausing occasionally to appraise some vegetables, or to pass her fingers over coloured silks not "sensible" enough to buy. We walk and munch on spicy Jamaican patties wrapped in brown paper towels. The woman Oma has bought them from knows her. She smiles broadly when she hands Oma her change, and says, "Now, you have a good week, gramma."

"Oma, what happened when Hitler came to power?" I ask.

"*Der* Hitler?" She frowns. "He didn't come to us."

"Nothing changed?"

"*Ha,* no. We had so much work to do, *nit.* We had no time for *des Politik-glump,*" she says, dismissing politics with a wave of her hand. "And then communism came, and they took everything away."

"But that was at the end of the war, Oma. What happened before that?"

"Before that was the *Hitlerzeit*," she says. Her tone says, haven't they been teaching you anything in that school?

"When did that start?"

"Well, the war started in '39. But we had nothing to do with it. Nothing. Only *Heimabends* we had. A woman was elected and she gave talks, and we all came together and sang songs about Germany, about the 'homeland.' That was during the *Hitlerzeit*."

"But, it didn't mean anything to you?" The insistence in my voice startles me.

"No, no," she says. "What could it mean? Most of us didn't even know where Germany was, we were so dumb."

"So nothing happened before the war came," I say.

"No, nothing at all, at all. There was the German-Hungarian Association, the *Hitlerjugend,* as they called it, for the young ones. It was like what they have here, Boy Scouts, you call it. They got together and sang, *nit,* and learned outdoors skills, to be disciplined, and had running races and things. Frank, he was nine or ten, he did that. Rudi would have too, if he hadn't had the accident with his foot.

"Once, there was a big meeting with boys from all over. The boys had to qualify to go, just like for the Olympics. Frank qualified, and I had to buy him new shoes for his uniform. They had to look sharp, *nit.* But these shoes were hurting him. He wasn't used to shoes, *nit,* so he took them off. The town boys laughed at him, they laughed until they started racing and Frank ran in his bare feet and beat them all. Won a little trophy for it even."

Oma stops in front of a display of cantaloupes on a fruit stand. Taking one in her hands, she brings it to her nose, and presses the end gently. It is not ripe, so she returns it to the pile.

"*Ja,* and then in 1940 some of the young men, they went to enlist. *Freiwillig*. Voluntarily. They thought they wanted to. They didn't have to go in the beginning, the war was far away. The war wasn't where we were."

In front of us is our final destination. The sign above the plain storefront says "European Meats." Underneath it in smaller letters is printed *Wurst und feinstes Fleish*—Sausage and finest meats.

The store is deep and narrow. Along one wall runs a glass display counter behind which four women work with quick, precise motions, slicing, weighing, and packaging. I realize that it has been years since I bought meat for myself. The heavy, wild aroma of smoked sausages fills my nostrils, and once more I feel five years old.

The store is busy as usual, and as Oma approaches the counter, I hang back, out of the way. In front of the counter is a tight throng of other Omas—short, solid women in head kerchiefs knotted tightly beneath their chins. Even though there is ample space behind them, they crowd up against each other, waving money in tight fists above their heads, lifting their voices, jostling to be served. I watch, bemused, as this age-old, imported ritual continues. If you wait, Canadian-style, for your turn, you will never get served in this store.

When Oma finally emerges, her arms are laden with packages wrapped in pinkish-grey paper. With a satisfied smile, she hands each package to me. She has bought Polish sausage, *Pressack,* and *Leberwurst,* ribs, pork fillets, and soup bones. I load everything into my rucksack and heft it onto my shoulders.

"*Gut,*" says Oma, "now we can go home."

ON THE WAY TO THE TRAIN, Oma leads me through a maze of quiet streets. She is tired, so we stop and sit on a bench in a tiny patch of green that passes for a park.

"*Schau'ma aweile,*" Oma says. Let's watch a while. An elderly man is moving his limbs in the slow dance of Tai Chi. Two skateboarders rumble past, their oversized pants threatening to fall off their hips, blondish hair in dreadlocks. Oma snorts.

"What kind of mother would let her children go out like that?" she scolds. "And that hair looks so stupid on the whites."

I laugh.

"What if I were to marry a black guy?" I ask.

"*Ha,* as long as you get along, that's great. But it will be difficult in this world," Oma replies. "As long as you are both ready for that."

A young mother chases after a wayward toddler. A middle-aged man in a white muscle shirt which barely covers his fleshy chest looks me up and down as he struts by, gold chains clinking. Oma follows him with her eyes. She leans towards me and says in a stage whisper, "That man should be wearing a bra." We cackle together over this for a while, and then slowly make our way back to Union Station. Oma buys her lottery tickets, and we wait for the train.

"WHEN THE SS CAME, they tried to stop us from shopping in the Jewish stores," Oma says pensively.

"When did they come, Oma?"

"Ha, maybe in '40? They were *grauslige Hunde*, the SS. We hated them, but we couldn't do anything against them. When they came, we were afraid to say anything, afraid they would lock us up or kill us. *Ja,* people started disappearing. *Die* Marie Windisch, her husband went to complain about something one day, and he never came back. Just like that.

"So then they started hanging around outside the Jewish stores. To hell with you, I thought at first, and went in anyways. You always got the best quality *bei die Juden.* So I kept going to them. But I kept my head down.

"And then one day the SS officer at the door had a stamp, and he was threatening to stamp everyone who went in on the forehead, with one of those stars, nit. He said if you went in, you were a sympathizer, that you were a Jew, too. I just stood there with my *Einkaufs* basket. I didn't know what to do. I could see into the store to where Herr Weiss sat behind the counter. His face was like stone. And then I saw Anna's face looking out from the curtain behind him. I started to go to her, but then our eyes met. She shook her head. Her eyes were so sad, so scared, and suddenly I thought of my children at home who needed me. And I didn't go in."

The train arrives, and we climb aboard. The wheels screech and the car rocks gently as we leave the station.

"*Ja,*" says Oma, "that's the last time I saw Anna. After that, we stayed away from St. Gotthard as much as we could. It was crawling with those Nazis. And then one day I had to go into town, and they were gone. All of the Jews were gone. In the Weiss store was already a Hungarian selling things. It was as if they'd never been.

"No one would say where they were taken. We didn't learn until after, a long time after everything was over, what the Nazis did with *die Juden*. They were good people, the ones I knew. Good people. Better than our people, some were."

We are silent. It strikes me that Oma has spoken her praise with uncomplicated sadness. Somehow, this matters to me. From my backwards-facing seat, I look out at the diminishing skyline of the city. The lake shimmers a cold silver under the gathering clouds.

Oma shifts in her seat. "But there were two," she says, "two Jewish men who owned a clock repair shop, and the people said that they would lure Christians into the dark back of the store and kill them and drink their blood."

"But Oma, you didn't believe that ... did you?"

"*Ha*," says Oma, laughing cryptically, "that's what people said."

Great-Oma

*O*MA AND I ARE SITTING on her bed, looking at family photo-graphs. The red maples outside the window are vibrant in the autumn rain.

"Oma, who's this?" I ask, pointing to a young woman captured in black-and-white tones turned sepia with age.

"Who? That's my mam."

I lift the album from my lap, and we examine the image together. The dress Oma's mother is wearing has a high, Victorian collar, a tightly cinched waist, and a skirt that reaches the floor, hiding her shoes. Her hair is up, but fine, soft curls at her temples have escaped the bun. Her gaze is calm, level. I would call her sophisticated were she not so young. She is posed with one hand resting on an ornamental wicker chair. On the chair is a potted palm.

"Where was she?" I ask.

"That was taken in Allentown," says Oma.

I look up from the photo. "Pennsylvania? I didn't know she'd been to America."

"*Ja,*" Oma explains, "she went when she was eighteen, nine-teen years old. To work. A few young people from our area went together."

"How long was she away?"

"Oh, I don't know." Oma shrugs. "A year? Two years maybe. It was a long trip."

I count back. The year was probably 1902 or 1903. What an adven-ture it must have been for her to travel so far from anything familiar. The world was so much bigger then. Did she wonder on that ship tossing in the middle of the Atlantic whether she would ever return? Imagine if she hadn't.

"Did she learn English there?" I ask.

"No, I don't think so. Well, I don't know for sure. They worked in a factory, with people from all over.

"My mam told only one story from that time. She went with her friends to the store to buy vinegar. They didn't know the English word for vinegar, so they brought the empty jar along. They tried with hands and feet to tell the shopkeeper what they wanted, but he just kept shaking his head saying, 'What you want, what you want?' So my mam, she takes the jar and sticks it under his hairy nose and says, '*Schmeck, du Wieniger Hund,*' and the shopkeeper says, 'Oh, you want a vinegar'!" Oma can barely form the words for laughter.

I look at her quizzically.

"*Wieniger Hund* is a bad thing to call someone," she explains, "but that's how they learned the word. Vinegar. *Wieniger.* Get it?"

A direct translation of *Wieniger Hund* would be Viennese dog. Ah, the creativity of German-speaking swearers. Dogs and pigs get a lot of play in derogatory phrases. *Du Schweinehund!* they yell in the stands at soccer matches. You pig-dog! Another translation I've found for pig and dog: bastard.

Oma finally stops laughing. "*Ja,* and you know what she brought back from Amerika?" she says. "My name. Laura. Your name too."

"Really?"

Oma nods. "She heard it and liked it. Maybe Laura was a friend, I don't know. So I was the only Laura in our whole *Gemeinde.*"

I look again into the quietly confident face in the photo. Who was this Laura? And why did Oma's mother go to America? To find a different life? To fall in love?

"So she came back and met my father and they were married," says Oma. "Then Emil was born, and me in 1912, and Mitzi two years later. Then in 1918 he fell in the war."

"Do you remember him, Oma?"

"Oh no, he had to enlist when I was two. We had no father growing up."

On the next page of the album is a photograph of Oma's mother and her five children. The soft lines of the American photo have vanished. Her features are sharper now, more like my mother's, and her eyes, unreadable. I feel sad.

"Oma, where was your mother from?"

"*Ha,* I don't really know. Her name was Theresia Cseh, and there were no Csehs in Burgenland. I think her family came from Czechoslovakia somewhere." She waves vaguely.

Pointing to the handsome young man with his hand on his mother's shoulder, Oma says, "Emil, he left for Amerika when he was eighteen. The photo was taken just before he left, the last time we were ever all together.

"That was in 1928, just in time for the Depression. He sometimes wrote letters home about living in boxcars on trains. He wrote from here and there, it sounded so exciting to us, so far away."

Two girls stand on either side of their mother in identical cotton-plaid dresses, their round faces grave. Oma has to show me which one she is. The other girl is Mitzi.

"Mitzi and I, we did everything together. School, dancing, everything. When she was sixteen she moved to Budapest, to work in the factory there. I missed her. *Ja,* I missed her a lot. You see those earrings she's wearing?"

I peer at the photo and nod.

"Opals. So beautiful. She gave them to me when she moved away."

"What happened to them?"

Oma shakes her head. "Lost. When the Russians came, we all took our earrings out because it was said that if they catch you, they'll rip them off, ear and all.

"By the time Emil left, our mam was already living with *der* Petok. Karl. They weren't married, *nit,* because Mam would have lost my dad's pension. There were lots of women like that after the first war. And so Milli was born, and Resi," Oma says, pointing to the little girls by her mother's knees in the photo.

"Right from the beginning Milli thought she was better than the rest of us. She was beautiful, and would come home in her fancy clothes with her rich boyfriends and I would come out of the barn with cow

Dreck on my dress and no shoes on. So come and help, I used to say, and she would get so embarrassed." Oma chuckles.

I think of Milli sitting in the bar she runs in a seedy part of Buffalo, New York, patting the brassy blond curls of her wild signature wig. A few years ago, Milli dragged Oma off for a week in Las Vegas. Oma wouldn't admit she'd had fun.

"Milli, *ja,* Milli is a story all by herself," says Oma, shaking her head.

"Now, Resi and I, we understood each other well. Especially during the war, it was so good to have her."

I picture Resi as I saw her in Budapest, in her wheelchair, straining to speak after her stroke. What I remember most vividly is the way she deep-fried all the food, even the cauliflower and broccoli. Her sour, brute of a husband with his suspected secret-service ties sat in his stained undershirt and glared at us the whole time.

"So, and after Resi and Milli were born, *der* Petok died."

"He died, too?"

"*Ja,* he was so choleric, a hot tempered man, and one day the barber came and cut his hair and gave him a shave, and just when he was finished, *der* Petok fell out of the chair and was dead. Heart attack. And she was alone again."

"So it started with her then," I say.

"Oh no, she never knew her father either. My grandfather died early.

"And my grandmother, she didn't even know her own birthday. 'You want to know how old I am?' she always said. 'Then ask my little finger. It knows. It's as old as I am'."

My mind is a whirr. Four. That makes at least four generations of women whose husbands, sometimes multiple husbands, died young. And four generations of fatherless daughters.

"So," I say, "I'd better not get married."

"What? Oh, no, you can't think like that." Oma's laughter is hollow.

Der Luftangriff

O MA AND I ARRIVE at Tante Frances and Onkel Frank's place just
as the fiery golds and reds of the northern autumn dissolve
into evening grey. Clouds are moving in, and the air smells of rain. I
breathe deeply, relieved to have left the city smog. It's no wonder that
Frank and Frances moved to their cottage when he retired.

When Frank rounds the corner of the cottage, he is wearing his
usual faded, plaid flannel shirt, and the smile beneath his fishing cap
is almost gleeful. I help Oma ease herself out of the car. She winces
as she straightens; she will be stiff tomorrow from the drive but
won't let on.

"So, you made it," Frank says, and kisses his mother.

"Oh, *ja*, Laura, she's a good driver," Oma says. "She doesn't drive
so wild like her mother."

Frank clomps over in his rubber boots and puts his hands on my
shoulders. "So, here's my girl!" he says and hugs me soundly. I sense
him looking over my shoulder toward the car.

"So, and where's Erika?"

"My mother? At home."

"Oh. She never comes," Frank grumbles, though he knew she was
not planning to visit. "I ask and ask and she never comes. I dunno
what her problem is."

I shrug and pick up Oma's bags.

Frances comes out to the porch, wiping her hands on her apron.

"Hallo, hallo!" she calls. "You've brought the rain with yous. Come
on in." She holds the door open, letting warm light spill out into the
darkness. The first big drops are falling as Frank takes Oma's arm
and I haul the bags inside.

Soon we are sitting in the living room, sipping hot chocolate and listening to the rain pound on the tin awnings. Frances passes Oma a blanket for her knees. Oma looks away from the dark window and shivers.

"Frank, what does that rain noise make you think of?" Oma asks.

He looks at her blankly.

"It makes me think of *der Luftangriff.* Maybe you don't remember."

"Oh, I remember the air strike, all right," Frank says, nodding slowly. "When they came with their war planes and bombs. Must have been in '42 they came."

Frances yawns and gets to her feet.

"Well, that didn't take long," she says.

"What?" Frank asks. Frances squeezes his shoulder and wishes us good dreams. "Try not to talk all night."

"So, *ja,*" Frank continues when she has left, "they came and bombarded us. You couldn't go out in the fields, they were shooting at us all the time…"

"Who?" I ask.

"The English. Or whoever was in there, they could have been Canadians or Americans. It didn't matter who; we hated them. Now, you only hear one side of the story. What we went through in those war times, you could write a whole book without even stopping."

I smile at him and take a sip of hot chocolate. "Did they bomb often?"

"Oh, *ja,*" Oma says, "every day. They shot and they threw bombs down. Not in our village, not in the houses but in the forest. In the forest and out in the fields the bombs landed."

"Why?"

"Ha, they just tossed them out and didn't know where they were landing. It wasn't like now, like over in the desert where the Americans have those smarter bombs, no. But the *Bahnhof,* the railway station in St. Gotthard was bombed. No trains could run because the tracks were also bombed. It was *furchtbar,*" she says, drawing out the vowels for emphasis. Dread–ful.

"We always ran inside when they came," Frank says. "Do you know where to go if bombers are coming? You stand in the corners, because they say when the bombs fall, there the walls are thicker, and they don't fall in as easily."

Oma nods gravely.

"What about the cellar?" I ask.

"*Ja* there too, if there was time," she says. "When we heard them coming, the soldiers ran here and there, and we ran into the corners, into the *Keller,* and everywhere, *nit.* They went buuuuuh with their guns, and then were gone again, and then in a little while they came again, five or six in a row. And then they shot, burburburburbur and threw the bombs down." She stabs her fingers at me in time with the shooting.

"That was the *Luftangriff.* That's how they bombed so much in Germany. All the cities were completely destroyed. But where we were there was not much, mostly fields, *nit,* but the *Bahnhof* in Gotthard, that they hit. *Ja,* that's how it was."

"Were there ever any English soldiers on the ground where you were?" I ask.

"No, they were in the air. They were on the ground up in Austria, where your Opa was captured, in Gmunden, that's where the English held the German and Hungarian troops captive. Those weren't so *grausly,* they didn't do anything cruel to the people, not like the Russians who raped the women and such, they didn't do this."

Oma pauses, considers. "It is possible though. I wasn't up there, *nit.* But you didn't hear anything about the English. They were good fliers, they bombed well," she says with undisguised admiration. "And the Americans were there, too, and the Canadians. Here from Kitchener, we know one, he also flew as a Canadian and bombed his own people. He took part in the bombing."

"So did my Grandpa Taylor," I remind her.

"*Ja,* he was out there, too. But not where we were, no." She shakes her head. "No, somewhere in Germany."

We sip our hot chocolate in silence. The rain has intensified.

"In '44, four or five weeks before Erika was born," Frank begins again, "there was no one in the house, just me and my mam. She was carrying water for the horses, for drinking, and it was too heavy for her. In the middle of the yard she fell down under the strain. I thought she was gonna die. Do you remember still?"

Oma nods.

"I harnessed Rigo," Frank continues, "put Mam on the wagon and drove to St. Gottard, to the doctor. He fixed her up and laid her on the wagon again. And then just when we were half way out of St. Gottard, the aeroplanes came again. Just when we got to the river, the sirens went, and there was a bridge, and I could see them coming. We were right at the bridge, on the side of the bridge, and they were shooting at us, at the bridge. So I drove the horse into the field, and there was a barn, and I drove Mama right in there. And then we hid in there. They were shooting at the bridge, on and on. Yeah. The bombing went on and on."

"And you were twelve?"

"Yes," Frank nods, "just about."

The rain adds a fourth voice to the conversation. I wonder if Frances can sleep.

"The worst was when they shot that train up," Oma says. "There were soldiers being transported in the train. And the *Flieger* came, the English, and they shot that train up. They flew as low as the trees right over our yard. And then, where our fields almost met the river, there was the small station, and there the train was standing. They shot it up completely. They were all dead, the poor soldiers, they were Hungarian soldiers. And then they carried lots of them to us, because we were the closest house. And the English used bullets that, when they hit you, everything was poisoned. You had to die. Some of the soldiers jumped into the river, but they died too.

"We had seven or eight in our house who were still sort of breathing, and we laid them in the kitchen, in the children's room, on my bed. *Tol is das Herz ausacaengt, tol ist die Lungen ausacaengt, hint hat oalles ausacaengt....* How we tried to stuff hearts and lungs and intestines back in. You wouldn't believe how bad it was. They all died. The soldiers from the town collected them all—there was no doctor who could have sewn them up or helped them, *nit*—they all died, and they were all gathered and put on a wagon, and transported to Gotthard, where they were buried, or something."

I don't remember when I first heard this story. I must have been five, six years old. If anything, Oma tells a less graphic version now than the one I recall.

"It took a long time to clean up all the blood in our house. And I washed the bed sheets, I boiled them, *nit,* but in the end I had to burn them. I was sure I could still smell the blood." She shakes her head slowly. "It was *furchtbar. Furchtbar.* Dreadful like you can't imagine. *Der Luftangriff.*"

School

I PAUSED WITH MY HAND ON THE CRANK while Oma poured the next handful of hazelnuts into the grinder. From the gadget attached to the edge of the kitchen table, a filigree of nut shavings cascaded into the bowl. It was my first weekend home from university. We were making a hazelnut-chocolate loaf. Oma was determined that I not go back to the residence unprovided for. I might starve.

The shower upstairs began to run. My mother was getting ready for work.

"Hope it's baked in time for Mom to take some with her," I said.

"*Ja,*" said Oma, "she should eat some before she goes. They never have time to eat on that aeroplane."

On the counter lay my mother's security pass: Flight Service Personnel, Air Canada. Issuing date, 15 March 1965. Beside it was a pile of German coins.

"Is she going to Frankfurt this week?" I asked. One month away at university and already I was out of touch.

Oma shrugged. "*Ja,* I think. Or maybe Munich."

The hazelnut shavings were spilling over onto the table. I stopped to gather them up.

"What do you have to learn at this university?" Oma asked. "*Lesen, Schreiben,* two plus two?"

"Oh, Oma." I sighed. But I was not sure how to answer. I abandoned my hazelnuts long enough to pull out some course texts and lay them on the table. *Concepts in Zoology. Fundamentals of Philosophy. Jane Eyre.* She flipped through them, stopping at the pictures of earthworms, *Lumbricus terrestris,* copulating.

"*Ee kenn mi do nit aus.* I can't follow any of this. *Des musst du alles wissen?*" she asked, weighing the books in her hands.

"Yeah, I have to learn most of it, I guess."

"Why?" she asked.

I had no answer for her.

"Did you like school, Oma?"

"*Ja,*" she said, emptying the nut shavings into the mixing bowl, "I liked to go, but I didn't learn everything they wanted me to. Nature studies and natural history I didn't like."

"Why not?"

"I don't know. I said, I don't need this. *Rechnen und Lesen und Schreiben* I could do well, and geography. I knew everything on the map, what this is and that. We had two big maps, no, three. One of Europe, one of Hungary, and a small one of Germany. Maybe we had one of the world, I don't know any more." She hesitated a moment. "I wish now that I had learned it better. There is much I wish I knew," she said.

I pictured her as a child, turning a defiant face from the blackboard to stare out the window at the fields or the clouds. Stubby nose, drooping socks. Oma the rebel.

"Your mother, now she was clever in school," Oma observed. "So clever. You know Waltraud, her friend? They were both the smartest in the class, smarter than all the boys. They would trade back and forth for the *Einz* in all their classes. The Germans, the real ones, they were always mad, they were jealous that a *Flüchtlingskind* was doing better than they were. It's not right that the refugees are in school with our children, they complained, but there was only one school in Pleidelsheim, *nit,* so they all went together. Oh, *ja,* she was smart. She knew everything. And the teacher loved her. Gave her one of his special books to take when we left."

I know something of your school story, Mom. At least on this side of the Atlantic. A long time ago, you told me this story:

At the knock, you close your book and slip from your attic room at Frank and Frances's house to investigate. Your brother Frank opens the front door when you are halfway down the stairs.

"Hello, you must be Mr. Binder," says a bright, gentle female voice from

beneath the brim of a brown felt hat. A familiar voice. Unexpected, out of context. Resisting the impulse to rush down to greet her, you let yourself sink noiselessly onto the step. The August evening air stealing in through the open door carries the earthy, chill breath of fall. You pull your skirt tightly over your knees, hug Frances's cardigan close around you, and watch as your brother takes Mrs. Allan's jacket and hat.

Frank left Germany for Canada when he was eighteen. You were only six. Seven years passed before you and Oma joined him in his house in Scarborough. He must have seemed like a stranger to you then. Even now he seems so much older, too old to be your brother.

From your perch on the stairs, you can survey the whole of the tiny house. You watch as Mrs. Allan steps into the front room, watch her taking in the modest surroundings. The cuckoo clock with its royal-blue carved birds, ticking self-importantly on the wall. The plastic crucifix, strung with rosary beads. The little oil painting of purple Bavarian mountains rising from synthetic green forests.

Frances comes bustling from the kitchen, drying her hands on her apron. Her attractive young face is flushed, apologetic. Has Mrs. Allan eaten, she inquires. Yes, thank you. With the four adults, the kitchen is full now, and warm with the lingering scent of Gulasch and boiled potatoes.

Four adults? Yes, four. Oma must have been there, perhaps helping her daughter-in-law with the dishes or wiping the stovetop. I see her standing in shadow by the kitchen doorway, hesitating. Teachers are important people, people to be respected, honoured. And here was her own daughter's teacher come to visit.

Oma steps forward to greet her. I see a smile pass across Oma's face, almost shy, as Mrs. Allan extends her hand.

You know, of course, why she has come. You wonder what your mother and Frank will have to say, not daring to hope.

"I WENT TO SCHOOL WHEN I WAS SIX," Oma continued, "for six years. We learned Hungarian and *Deutsch*. But more *Deutsch*. We had only two hours of Hungarian in the week. The government let us Austrians alone back then, before the war. It was only after, after 1920, that we belonged to Hungary, *nit*. And we learned reading and writing and math, geography and everything else, too. It was good. But each week the priest would come twice and teach. Catechism. You know what that is? And History."

"What was the priest like?" I asked.

"*Oh, er war gut*," she says and chuckles. "*Oh, ja*, he was good, *aber wenn er hab ist gwesen hat er uns immer herkaun.*"

"He did what?"

"He would beat us. Only when he was mad." She laughed. "When we saw him coming we would always yell, *Der Pfoarrer kommt, der Pfoarrer kommt, nit,* and when he heard this, he would cut a switch and come searching for us. Who was yelling 'the priest is coming?' he said. We hid behind the schoolhouse, or bent over our books and pretended we didn't hear.

"He always had on brown pants and this black robe. And his hair was so thin and white that you could see every wrinkle on his scalp. When he was mad at us, we knew it because his whole head went red, poppy red. Especially this one purple spot just behind his ear, shaped like, just like, the Budapest on the map. And you could see one vein, thick as a worm, pulsing down the middle of his forehead.

"And then he would go into the bushes and cut a long switch. The closest boy would get it. Not hard, though, I don't think. He didn't mean it this way, *nit.*

"But he was a good priest," she added, still smiling.

Mrs. Allan, Margaret Allan, was your self-appointed guardian angel, you've told me, Mom. When you arrived in Canada a year and a half earlier with not a trace of English on your tongue, the school in Scarborough had not known what to do with you. Because you were thirteen, they put you in a Grade Eight class. But it was the remedial class, the class for slow learners. When you realized how you had been labelled, you let yourself slouch low in your seat, and vowed not to open your mouth, ever. Wrote long, frustrated letters to Waltraud.

When you had asked your teacher in Germany how you could prepare yourself for the move, he had replied with great solemnity, "You must learn how to skate. Everyone in Kanada skates." That was it, probably all he knew about the unimaginably vast landmass coloured pink on his classroom map.

Mrs. Allan was a gentle soul. I see her slim figure turning from the blackboard to address the class, her face framed by wispy, light-brown hair escaping from a French twist. Young, idealistic, and so very kind. Almost immediately, she spotted the intelligence behind your wretched silence. Mrs. Allan became your English tutor. And you devoured the words as quickly as she could introduce them, hungry for the language that would break your isolation. Hungry for friends closer than an ocean away.

You still write to Waltraud, don't you? But I can't think of anyone over here that you are close to like that, no woman at least. Why? You speak better English now than most people I meet.

In the summer after school was out, Mrs. Allen would have you over to her house once a week for lessons and lunch. That first Tuesday, when you boarded the bus that would take you across Scarborough, you held your lesson book tightly to your chest. Tucked inside it was a note from Frank for the bus driver, indicating your destination should you get lost. "Like a three-year-old child you treat me!" you said to Frank when he pressed it into your hand. But as the streets lost their familiarity, you were glad to have it.

Mrs. Allan always welcomed you with a smile and a hug. She made sure you knew how delighted she was that you had come. At the lunch table, the conversation perplexed and delighted you.

"Ian, honey, would you pass the butter? Christopher, mind you don't spill the sugar!" Mrs. Allan would say to her little boys. And then suddenly, you would be sugar. "Thanks, sugar." With a smile. "Zucker?"

Sometimes they would break into song. "Sugar in the morning, sugar in the evening, sugar at suppertime..." Or, "My bonnie lies over the ocean, my bonnie lies over the sea..." And you would sing along, belonging. Content, for once, not to understand.

WHEN WE FINISHED WITH THE HAZELNUTS, Oma unwrapped a big block of semi-sweet chocolate. I turned it on edge and began to saw into it with a sharp knife. The chocolate crumbled into slivers and chunks, dark and decadent. I furtively popped choice chunks into my mouth.

Oma grinned at me. *"Iss na, iss."* Eat, eat.

"What was your teacher like, Oma?" I asked. Oma rested her swollen, knotted fingers, watching my progress.

"The teacher was good," she said, "and fair, but the students were so *umgeschickt,* so difficult. We had some *Findelkinder,* orphans, those who had no one and were taken in by the people, and they were so nasty, so mean to the teacher. They would smash in his windows, steal his things. And so he always gave them a good beating.

"When we went home after school, we had to form up, two by two, in a long line. I was always beside KnaunzMichael, and I tried hard not to look at him. Ever." Oma wrinkled her nose.

"Because he was an orphan?" I asked.

"No, not because he was an orphan. Because he smelt like a chicken coop, and he was always trying to take my hand. I used to think that if I looked into his little red chicken eyes he would ask me to marry him."

"How old were you?"

"Oh, about eight, I guess." She smiled. "The teacher stood in the doorway of the school and could see the whole length of the village. You know how small it is. And so off we marched, two by two. When one of us wandered out of the line, or pushed and shoved, we were punished the next day, if the teacher remembered. And if someone came past us, a man or a woman, then we had to greet them, *Gelobt sei Jesus Christus,* and if we didn't do this, then he scolded us.

"Remember Luisa, my friend? She married him. KnaunzMichael. After the war, they moved to Buffalo and had eleven children. She's dead now, though."

Holding the red mixing bowl steady, I stirred carefully as Oma poured a rocky chocolate river into the pale batter.

"Did you have the same teacher for the six years?"

"No, at the beginning we had the old teacher, Mayer, *der Mayerlehrer.* He was a good teacher.

"I didn't want to go to school on the first day, I remember. My mother put ribbons in my hair, and she made me promise not to get dirty, to sit up straight, to be very, very good. This scared me, so I hid in the pantry behind the pickled eggs and the beets. My feet hurt. I had only my Sunday shoes to wear, and my socks were scrunched up under my toes. I imagined my shoes were filling up with blood, and that they would spill if I took a step.

"Then he came, the teacher, and said, '*Kiem na* Laura, come on.'

He was a nice man. Always greeted my mother. Asked after our dad. I think he was the man dressed up as St. Nickolaus before Christmas. He lived right in the village, and the school was right there too."

"Oh," I said, "it was that house, wasn't it, the house with the chestnut tree in the front?" A plain little structure when I saw it in 1993, not discernibly different from those beside it. But the chestnut tree, already old in Oma's childhood, still holds the whole house in its magnanimous shade. I can see the generations of little boys, barefoot, knickers cut from a father's old pair, stuffing their pockets with smooth chestnut weapons.

"We had just one room with the six classes in it, we were not many children. He taught me well, though, everything."

"So he made you come to school on the first day?"

"No," she smiled, "then my friend Luisa came and took my hand and said, *Kiem na kiem*, come, come on, and then we went."

The batter resting, we greased the baking pans with fingerfuls of vegetable shortening, our hands working smoothly over the tins.

"And then *der Mayerlehrer* got too old," Oma continued, "and we got a new teacher, a young teacher, and he was so big, but so dumb. From him we learned nothing. That one just taught us about the insects, and about the mice and the rats and the worms, *lauter des Zeug*, things like that," she said disdainfully, banishing him with a flick of her greased fingers. I glanced at my zoology textbook and grinned: Nematods, Annelids, Platyhelminthes — whole Phyla squirming and writhing across its pages.

"He was so tall and thin, like a stork. His arms stuck out of his jacket like, you know, those clothes hangers. I never saw that man without a book. He would be walking along and suddenly, it was so strange, he would crouch down in some garden and he would look and look, and write in his little book. The boys used to plan to steal that book, *nit, aber er hat mir Leid getan, wirklich,* so sorry I felt for him. He would have to marry his book, I could see, for no one would have such a one. He was not there long, perhaps a year, then he had to go to the war."

I turned the oven on, and began to clean up the bits and pieces of our project.

"Oma, your father was in that war too, wasn't he?" I asked.

She nodded. "He never came back."

The voices in Frank's kitchen reach you as a dull murmur. You don't try to make out the words, but snippets drift up, unbidden.

"But Mr. Binder, you must see the importance —" Mrs. Allan says.

"Yes, Ich weiss, but, there are — wie sag ich das? — needs, you know..." Frank pastes his words together haphazardly. From the bedroom come Frank Junior's teething screams. Frances rises to comfort him, shifting her again swollen frame from the room. Frank follows her with his eyes.

"How I gonna be able to support..."

Your fingers trace the raised, swirling patterns in the green velour wallpaper. The chill is still seeping in under the door, and it is dark on the stairs now. The yellow light from the kitchen seems far away.

You managed, with your teacher's help, to finish your Grade Eight year on time to graduate with the "normal" Canadian children. Mrs. Allan was thrilled with your progress, and her talk had been full of high school all summer. Now there were two short weeks left before classes would start. Registration day had come and gone.

"No, she is not too young. Mensch, I was working already two years when I was fifteen," says Frank, throwing up his hands for emphasis, and you know that the conversation is over.

Mrs. Allan is gracious enough as he helps her into her jacket. But as she turns to leave, she happens to raise her eyes, and they meet yours. They are full of an anger, of a helpless frustration so intense that it is all you can do not to look away.

It was just the times, you tell me now. It wasn't his fault. We needed the money, Frances soon had Frankie, Linda and Karen in that tiny house. Even after we dug out the basement, we were living on top of each other. I don't blame him.

Mom, I do. Grade Eight, Frank decided, was more than enough education for a girl in 1960. How could he? A part of me cannot forgive his lack of foresight, no matter how logically you present it.

You claim you can't remember what Oma had to say about all of this. The way you tell it, she didn't involve herself at all. This may be, but I can't believe she didn't care. After so many years of having her life dictated by the whims of war governments and the struggle for basic necessities, I don't think she would have imagined that she could impact the course of your future. I see her shrug heavily. "Ha, what can we do?" she says. You might not have heard the sadness in her voice. But I'm sure it was there.

When I come home now, it is Oma who squeezes me hardest. I was raised on Oma-hugs. Enveloping, rib cracking, full. I get the feeling that her hugs have improved with age. Watching you with her, the way you hold each other at a distance, maybe brushing your lips against her cheek to say goodbye, I feel you have missed out. If anything, I imagine it was even more difficult for you two to show each other love when you were a teenager.

When I hug you, I feel big, bulky, as though I will crush your slender frame. An oak hugging a reed.

"WHEN THE SCHOOL HOLIDAYS CAME," said Oma, "the parents all had to come to the school, and the priest was there, and the teacher, and the mayor, and they watched to see who knew everything the best. It was another day for hair ribbons and clean shoes. I hated that day every year. The adults all looked constipated, especially the farmers in their Sunday suits. They still smelled of manure, all crammed into the little room. They don't know anything anymore that is not grain or pigs or cows, I thought.

"And the women, they would watch each other. Not directly, *nit*, but I saw them looking at each other's dresses, at who had stockings on.

"The priest, not the teacher, asked the questions. We had to know Catechism, *nit*, and spelling and adding. Then he would point to the map, where is this and this, he would ask, and we had to say. And he always hit around with his stick, if you knew or if you didn't. *Du kannst gut*, he said, and hit the *Schuler* across the back with his stick."

"Why?" I had to ask.

"Why?" Oma lifted her open hands, shrugged her shoulders. "*Hah*, that was his style, he didn't mean it that way. He asked a few children where Sarajevo was and they didn't know, and he hit them. I knew it so well—"

"You still remember that?"

"*Ja*, Sarajevo it was. I knew it so well, but I sat still and looked down. Then his brown pants were there, beside me, and he took the pointer and lifted my chin up so I had to look at him. And I did. Looked him right in the eye. That worm in his forehead was pulsing, but I didn't care. He gave me his pointer, and I went to the map, and I pointed to it. Sarajevo. Right at it. I saw my mam, standing by the door, all in black. She smiled at me, I remember, and I knew she was proud."

"Then he took the stick back and said, 'I knew you knew it,' and hit me with it. Hard. On my shoulder, on my head, on my hand. Oh, I was mad," she said, but was laughing again.

"But Oma, he sounds like a horrible man, why didn't the parents do something?"

Oma just shook her head, laughing at me.

"And so school was over," she said. "After school we had to herd the cows out onto the meadows, and we had to look after them, and we played. And then with twelve years I went to St. Gotthard, to work."

"To work?"

"*Ha ja* to work."

"Oma, I was almost twelve before you would even let me ride the bus alone."

Oma nodded slowly. "*Ja,* this is a different world," she said. "Here, I worry about you."

"You worry about everything," I said, trying to suppress my irritation.

"*Ja,* what else can I do?" said Oma, raising her hands.

"Oma, did anyone have a chance to go on, to do more school?"

"*Ja,* some went to the *Hochschule* in Gotthard, but only the teacher's children, and the doctor's. Mitzi, my little sister, she was smart and she went. But after a year they sent her back. Farmers, they told us, should stay farmers. It was from the state, from the Hungarian government, these rules. We were lucky they let us go until Grade Six.

"Oh, but the doctor's children were so dumb. I knew everything much better. It was like that. Nothing we could do about it."

This is not the end of the story. In the days after Mrs. Allan's visit, you start searching for a better job than the corner five-and-ten where you had been putting in hours stuffing used toys for re-sale. There is talk, too, of an old Hungarian gentleman in Toronto looking for a housekeeper, a live-in companion. Your mother decides to visit and consider the job, to see if he has space for both of you. And one evening, you board a bus that will take you deep into the city. Again you are on your own, carrying directions, but from Mrs. Allan this time. I see you, a slight, earnest figure, blond hair pulled back, mouth set in a firm line, entering the halls of Jarvis Collegiate. I see you walking up to the secretary and saying, in careful, planned English, that you would like to enrol. Night classes — Grade Nine.

Five years you attended. How many nights a week? Juggling studies with full-time work. No help at home, I imagine. But encouragement, I hope. That Grade Twelve diploma gathering dust in some basement box means more to me than any degree I'll ever earn.

OMA PEERED INTO THE OVEN at the baking hazelnut-chocolate loaf. She straightened stiffly and looked at the clock.

"I hope it's finished before your mother has to leave," she said. She sat down across from me, heavily. "Promise me you'll never become a flight attendant."

"Oh, I don't know," I mused. "It wouldn't be bad for a while…"

"No. Don't do it."

Her vehemence surprised me.

"I worry," Oma continued, "I worry every time she goes up in one of those aeroplanes that she won't come back. I've often said to her, what will happen if you don't come back. Then your child will have no one, no mother and no father. A girl needs her mother. *Ja*, that's what I worry. Especially when you were still small."

"Oh, Oma," I said, smoothing the tablecloth. "You worry too much."

"*Ja*, I worry. I worry about you. That you aren't eating enough away at that university. Look how your collarbone is sticking out! And you dress like it's *Hoch-Sommer* in the middle of the winter, look how your belly shows. Stay warm, *i sogs dir*. You don't believe me now, but when you're my age and full of arthritis you'll regret it. Your mother should teach you these things better."

I pulled my T-shirt down and said nothing. My ride back to university would be coming in two hours.

"Your mother's teacher in Germany," said Oma, "he took me aside after church in the weeks before we left. He said to me, Erika is a very smart girl. If she were to stay in Germany," she said slowly, "she would study and become a teacher."

I took the loaf from the oven and set it on a cooling rack. When I returned to the table, Oma was wiping her eyes with a tissue.

"*Ja,* a teacher. My Erika."

WHILE THE LOAF COOLED, I lay on my stomach on the bed in my mother's room and watched her pack for work. When I was little, I used to do this every time she left. Kneeling on the floor in her white bathrobe with her hair wrapped up in a towel and surrounded by mini bottles of shampoo, she reminded me of some new-age priestess performing a ritual. The packing ritual. She was wrapping each bottle in a plastic bag. You can never be too careful, she'd taught me time and again, you never know what might spill. I stretched out my arms and yawned loudly.

"That university life certainly seems to tire you out," my mother said. "Try to get more sleep, will you?"

"Mmmhmm." I nodded, swallowing another yawn.

She looked at me critically. "But you've really slimmed down, *gell*? You're looking good."

I raised my eyebrow, but she was already rolling a sweater to pack, and did not look up.

"So, are you enjoying your studies?" she asked.

I shrugged. "Too early to say. I think so."

My mother laughed. "You should have heard Oma on the phone the other day with Frau Schnoltzer, bragging about you."

"About what?"

"About how 'her girl' is at university, about how smart you are."

I sat up slowly and pulled my T-shirt down again. "Oh."

In silence, I watched as my mother filled the suitcase's small dimensions to capacity, tucking socks into shoes, filling empty pockets with rolled shirts. She has her System—everything has its place. If it's too empty, she maintains, everything will slide around and get wrinkled. She always lays the top half of her pants in the bottom like a liner, puts everything else on top, then folds the legs over so they don't get creased. Somehow, especially when I was little, there was always space left for her to bring back chocolate or small presents.

"Did you ever want to go?" I asked.

"To university?" She shrugged. "What I wanted never mattered. Keeping food on the table mattered."

"Oma hates your job," I said.

She snorted. "I know. She's good at disapproving. Always has been." She wrapped a nightgown around her curling iron. "Did you know I was your age when I got this job?" she asked.

I nodded. "You were going to be a teacher back in Germany, eh?"

Her hands paused their folding. She looked at me. "Oh, really?"

"Yeah. If you'd stayed. Oma tells me the teacher had big plans for you. She cried just now, telling me about it."

My mother snapped her suitcase closed and sunk onto the bed beside me. Letting the towel fall from her hair, she sighed. "I had no idea," she said. "No idea."

Advice

*I*T IS SEVEN O'CLOCK on a Friday evening, and the little girl jumps up from the table to turn on the ancient television. The girl's mother is away at work, so her Oma has made pancakes for dinner. The girl's fingers are still sticky from the jam and applesauce that has oozed from the thick, rolled crepes, and she wipes them on her overalls. "Today your mother's not here," Oma has said with glee. "Today we can eat with our hands."

The little girl claps as Oma's favourite show comes on. Oma passes her granddaughter a wet cloth to wipe her hands, and they sit giggling together as Beau and Luke Duke send their orange car leaping across gullies with police cruisers in hot pursuit. Their laughter is conspiratorial; the girl knows better than to tell her mother they have watched *The Dukes of Hazard* again. "What are you thinking," her mother had yelled at Oma, "letting a five-year-old watch such violence?"

When the show is over, Oma switches to the only other channel and fiddles with the dials until the bits of light on the screen arrange themselves into distinguishable shapes——chairs, dresses, faces. There are figures dancing across the screen, dancing in and out of colour, in and out of the electrical snowstorm of reception. When the sound kicks in, an accordion and brass band begins a rousing German folk chorus, and on cue, the red-faced men in *Lederhosen* and breathless women in tightly-laced *Dirndls* all raise their glasses of (what looks like) orange juice in a toast. Broadcast from Kitchener, the show is called *Ein Prosit* — Cheers.

Oma holds out her hand, and the little girl bows. Her feet on Oma's feet, her hands at Oma's hips they waltz and polka across the moss-green carpet, under the warm light of the crazy orange lamp.

Now, i wonder how that orgy of kitsch ever made it on air. But I also wonder where those dances were taking Oma as she swung her giggling grandchild around the room.

"EVERY SUNDAY WHEN I WAS YOUR AGE, maybe a bit younger," says Oma, "there was a dance." Oma and I are peeling carrots for the soup already simmering on the stove. I breathe in the warm, spicy smell of this simple beef and vegetable broth. I am glad when the soup clouds enough to hide the thick soup bones full of wobbly white marrow. When it is ready, Oma will spread this marrow on slices of rye bread and eat it. She will smack her lips and make a point of offering me some. At least this time we are alone. When I was little and had friends over for lunch, she would take each bone and run her tongue around its insides, sucking every bit of marrow out. *"Du woast ja nit wos guit is* — you just don't know what's good," she'd tease, winking at my friends and laughing at me.

"*Ja,*" Oma continues, "every Sunday there was a dance. One Sunday it was in our village, one Sunday in Fidisch, one Sunday in Radling.... We jumped on our bicycles and went where there was music. The *Gasthaus* in Jakobshof was across the street from our house — still is, you saw it. On Sundays, my sisters and I — Resi, Mitzi, even Milli was at home then — we would practice dancing with brooms and with each other. Polkas, waltzes around our little kitchen. Our mam, she watched us sometimes and clapped her hands. When the windows were open we would hear them start to play in the *Gasthaus,* and we would drop everything and run across the street to join the dance.

"People came from everywhere, from Radling, from Unterradling, from Fidisch...When they knew there was music we all came together. The musicians, they had violins, a clarinet, an accordion, a great big tuba. The tuba player, he would pass out halfway through the night. Too much drinking, not enough air. But the violins, the music...*wie sag ich das*? How do I say this?...was alive. You just had to dance."

Oma's eyes are bright. In my mind I take her face and smooth away the wrinkles, thicken and darken her wispy grey hair. I try to peel away the years, to see the young woman as her suitors saw her, radiant, standing ready for the dance.

"During *Faschingszeit*, the last days before Lent," she continues, "we started on Saturday, to play and to dance. And that went on until Monday morning—no one went home, no one slept. At dawn we changed our clothes and went straight to work."

Do you remember, Mom, when you showed me your dresses? Oma was at bingo, I think, because we were alone, sorting through the linen closet. When I close my eyes I can smell the fabric softener mustiness of that dim, close space. I pulled one of the brown suitcases out from under the shelves piled with cosy stacks of blankets and towels. You opened it, and carefully, almost reverently lifted out the dresses and laid them on the floor beside us. You unfolded them, one by one, shook out the years of creases, held them up to your kneeling frame, then to mine. The sleek black number with the bolero jacket and fake fur cuffs. The turquoise dress with the full skirt that held the ocean in its hues. I gingerly fingered the chiffon and taffetas, the soft underslips and sheer overskirts as though touching unknown creatures. Dancing dresses. You smiled gently as you watched me. "Yes, I lived to dance," you told me then. "Maybe you'll want to try these when you're older."

I never did try them on; they would never have fit. But I have thought about the girl who wore them. And I think I can see you, I can see the quiet young woman of sixteen, seventeen coming home to the grey house on Castlefield after a long day at the factory. A day of avoiding eyes that might ask "How do you do?" You are right, the question doesn't make sense. I see you shed the grey-blue uniform of the Dyment Limited factory, shed the language which still ambushes you with flips of meaning, twists of phrase. You slip out of the ill-fitting uniform, slip into the turquoise taffeta, and are transformed.

On Oma's shelf there is a photograph of you in a long, deep green gown, black gloves stretched past your elbows, your ash blond hair piled high in stylish sophistication. You are standing in an archway, looking past the camera as though you have just emerged from the dark unfocused place behind you. A princess, I used to think. A princess from another place.

That is how I picture you stepping onto the dance floor on those grey winter evenings at the German club on Sherbourne Street. And they love you, those men at the club, ten, fifteen years older, who spin and twirl you through polkas and jives, waltzes and twists. They hold you, a living part of the broken world they left in pursuit of their Kanadian dreams. And you laugh and flirt in the familiar cadences of that other world, the German words wrapping and shielding your dancing forms from the cold, lonely Toronto winter.

THE LITTLE GIRL IS SITTING CROSS-LEGGED on the floor watching her mother get ready for work, for her weekly trip to Frankfurt. Or Vienna, Zurich, maybe Düsseldorf. The carpet of the bathroom feels warm against the girl's skin. Yellow light from her mother's make-up mirror softens the brown geometric patterns on the walls. Her mother chose the wallpaper for the girl's father. She wanted him to have a masculine space, she says, in this house of women. The paper is beginning to peel now, and she talks of ripping it out, but the girl won't let her.

Leaning against the wall beside the toilet is a stack of books and magazines. *Chatelaine, Brigitte, House Plant Care. How to Dress Rich on Less.* This last one is part of a series: How to dress rich, decorate rich, and entertain rich — "on less."

Her mother steps into the smart lines of the navy-blue Air Canada uniform. She sits down at the make-up mirror and looks critically at her hair. The girl scrunches her eyes closed as a sticky mist of hair spray descends on everything. She plays with the eyelash curler, trapping and releasing her fingers.

"Come here, sweetie," her mother says. They look into the mirror together. The girl makes a face and they laugh. "You have your father's eyes, you know," her mother says, hugging her daughter close with one arm.

"Oh!" she exclaims, "I almost forgot to put on my lips!" The little girl giggles. Taking a lip pencil, her mother outlines her lips and then fills them in with wine-red lipstick. Just like a colouring book, her daughter thinks, don't colour outside the lines. She has never seen her mother outside the house without 'her lips on.'

"It's important," her mother says. "Once I was still in my morning coat when the doorbell rang. I was so embarrassed standing there looking a mess talking to the woman — she was selling something, or canvassing, I'm not sure. But that day I vowed never to face the world unprepared again. It's not an easy world, my *Schnuckele,*" she says, cupping her daughter's face in her hands, "You have to do what you can."

"OMA, DID YOU HAVE a lot of boyfriends?" I ask.

"Boyfriends?" says Oma, her peeling knife pausing briefly as she considers the question. "Boyfriends? I got along with everyone. Everyone liked me, and I danced with everyone, and I didn't go home with anyone. Just ours, the ones from our village, the ones I could trust, the ones I knew wouldn't do anything to me. But never with those from Fidisch or Oberradling. Oh, from Oberradling I had one, one who worked at the factory with me..." She pauses, smiles faintly.

"But it was not like here, boyfriend and girlfriend, where people smooch and neck *und des oalles,* and all that. We just walked home with them, after the dance. I had lots of, not directly boyfriends, but boys that liked me, liked to dance with me. I danced with everyone, even with the *Zigeuners,* the gypsies. The other girls didn't." She wrinkles her nose.

"There was one in Fidisch, *Zigeuner*Eddi. He was dark, and had eyes like coal. He wore this red embroidered sash around his waist, I remember, a gypsy sash that would move with him when he danced like a flag in the wind. He was a good dancer, but no one wanted to dance with him. Once we rode our bikes to Heiligen Kreutz where there was music, and *Zigeuner*Eddi was sitting alone, and I said to him, 'Eddi, why don't you dance?' 'Will you dance with me?' he asked. 'Of course,' I said, and then I held out my hands. We danced until we couldn't any more. After that, *Zigeuner*Eddi, he would always say, '*komm na,* Laura, *komm,* I know you'll dance with me.' And I would."

I see the red sash wrapping itself around and around the twirling couple. I hear spicy violins and giddy laughter and see dark eyes catching candlelight and I want to be there.

Oma gathers up the cleaned carrots and slips them into the cauldron.

"As I said, I was friends with everyone, I talked with everyone, there was no one too bad or too good—I just thought, once or twice doesn't matter. Just go dance with them, they are happy about it, and…you forget it. I was that way. And that is how you should be. Good with everyone."

"Just don't come home pregnant." This was the extent of Oma's advice to you in your dancing days. I picture you moving past each other in the house on Castlefield Street like familiar strangers.

I see you sitting alone in the dim basement, concealed by the hanging sheet forest of Oma's washing, rubbing your legs with a sandpaper glove because Oma disapproved of shaving. Or writing tortured letters to your best friend Waltraud across the ocean, scheming your return home. Or pouring over patterns for the dancing outfits Tante Frances would let you create on her Singer sewing machine.

You can laugh now when you tell me of those days in the house on Castlefield where Oma was housekeeper. But you were so painfully alone. I feel it through your laughter. Oma couldn't have been happy either. Why couldn't you talk to each other, help each other? What stopped you? Was it anger at being uprooted and dropped into the shallow soil of urban Ontario? Was it the crowd of ghosts your mother carried from an Austro-Hungarian village she still calls 'home,' a place you didn't remember and wanted nothing to do with? Or was it the memory of a German boy who smelled of sweet grass and milk waiting for you on the cemetery wall under the linden tree . . .

In the forest of sheets you pulled your sandpaper smoothed legs in to your chest and cried silently.

But you learned to hide tear-blotched skin with make-up, to wear bright lipstick and deep-blue eye shadow, to emphasize your high cheekbones with rouge. Just don't come home pregnant, your mother would say, and you would laugh.

THE GIRL, A TEENAGER NOW, has just told her Oma that she has a boyfriend. They are alone in the kitchen, eating leftover goulash for dinner. Oma's goulash is thick and hot. Chunks of tender stewing beef poke out of bright orange sauce.

"So?" Oma says.

"What, Oma?"

"So, have you kissed him yet?"

The girl smiles hesitantly. "Well…yes."

Oma puts her fork down. Straightens slightly. "Then it is about time you learned to cook."

The girl is suddenly aware of the intense paprika smell in the room, on her lips, in her mouth. She laughs and waits, curious to see what will happen next.

"This pill business, it's not a good idea." The girl blinks. "You know," Oma continues, "your mother took these pills for a while and then she had your brother. He died because of those pills." She speaks plainly, as if she were providing a basic recipe.

"Oma, that's not true," says the girl, finding her voice. Oma doesn't seem to hear.

"And abortion, it is so dangerous. You know, *bei uns da Hoam* some girls, they went to the gypsies to get rid of the life in their bellies, but they came back sick, very sick. Some died."

"But Oma, you don't think that I—"

"*Ha,* I know how it is. My friend Maria and I were the only girls in our village who had white weddings." She chews thoughtfully. "But your Opa, he insisted that *wir sollen uns ausprobieren* a week before the wedding. He wanted test it out to see, you know, if we fit."

"Oma!" the girl sputters. The paprika has set her mouth on fire. Shaking her head, she studies Oma's face. What a sweet little old lady, people say when they meet her. Sweet. They should try her goulash.

"So what do you think," the girl ventures, "it's OK to do it?"

"*Ha,*" Oma says, "let me tell you something. We were at a dance one Sunday, in Oberradling I think. And there was this big burly Hungarian man strutting around like this." Oma sticks her chest out and makes a bulldog face. "He thought he was so sexy, *nit,* and he was trying to get all the girls to dance with him. And then he pulled this thing out of his breast pocket, this little rubber thing, and started blowing it up. All of my girlfriends, they ran shrieking from the room. But I didn't go. I was curious, *nit,* and I wanted to figure out what it could be. I stood there and watched as his head went red with blowing. He stopped then, and looked at me with the vodka in his eyes. 'Go on, take it,' he said, 'take it.' But then my friend came running back to me and pulled me away and explained. And when I looked at the balloon again, I thought oh, I can see how that would work…"

"IT WAS A BEAUTIFUL DRESS, wasn't it?" the girl's mother says. She sits down beside her daughter and together they look at the grainy image of the woman in the green gown. "I borrowed it for that night. Look at that hairdo! Is that my hair all piled up like that? I guess it must be." She laughs and runs a hand over her stylish bob.

"Where were you going, Mom?" the girl asks.

"That was the Hungarian Ball, I think. But anyone could go. The picture, let me see…the picture was taken at the Royal York. Yes, that's right. And that German fellow took the photo. I knew him from the German dances. He spent most of that evening with me. Had a nice smile, I remember. And he was a good dancer, of course. And afterwards…" She hesitates, looks at her teenager thoughtfully. "Afterwards, he invited me back to his place. I decided to go."

"And?" The girl looks up from the photo.

"And I was curious. No one had ever invited me back before, and I guess I wanted to see…But nothing happened."

The girl raises an eyebrow. "Nothing?"

"Well, he started to kiss me, and in a rush I knew I didn't want him to. And then I went home," her mother says carefully.

"So, Mom, why are you telling me this?"

"I was lucky, Laura. I was stupid and lucky. Things are different now. I just want to say be careful." She brushes her daughter's cheek lightly with the back of her hand.

The girl sighs dramatically. "You've been talking to Oma, then."

Her mother stiffens. "Oh no," she exclaims, "What has she been telling you? No, wait." She raises her hand. "Sex is a duty, right? Something to be endured, not enjoyed. That you should wait, right?" She closes her eyes, shakes her head. "Well, it's not a good idea to wait for marriage, Laura. It is something I want you to experience —"

"Look," the girl interrupts, "why you two feel the need to tell me these things at this point is beyond me. I'm not stupid." She thinks of the summer before and the camp where she'd worked, of lying on the dock with her new friend in the darkness, watching for satellites and shooting stars. Of feeling his fingers trace the constellations on her skin.

"Laura?" her mother asks.

The girl starts, her mind returning to the conversation. "Just trust me on this, OK?" she says gently.

They are silent. The girl returns the photo to the shelf. As she turns to go, her mother catches her hand.

"I'll still worry," she says. "Even if they deserve your love…be careful. Be careful who you let love you."

Oma is adding spices to the soup; salt, pepper, paprika, the tiny flakes swirling on the liquid like a signature.

"Oma, the towns where you danced, some of them were far away, weren't they?" I ask, picturing the fields and woods punctuated by sleepy villages.

"Oh, *ja,* they were far. But it was different from here. No one had a car or *sauwos* like that. No. Only in St. Gotthard, the doctors each had a car, but no other person had one, only bicycles. And not everyone. In our village there were maybe four or five of us with bicycles. The others were farmers and they didn't go anywhere anyways, except to the dances. Then they would take horse carts, because they could trust the horses to take them home when they were too drunk." She pauses to raise a steaming cooking-spoonful of soup to her lips. Adds more pepper to the pot with a flick of her fingers.

"No, we had nothing like cars. It was very poor. But we were content, all of us, it was so nice, everything. I often came home from the dance in the middle of the night, alone, even through the forest. I had no fear. I could have no fear, *nit,* because no one did anything to you. We were stupid. So stupid, but we were happy. We didn't know anything, not like later. Later, things went on that you could never imagine." She spears through the marrow of a soup bone with a fork. "But before, we were happy. We didn't have to be afraid that someone would kill us or rape us or anything like that. *Sauwos hats nit gehm bei uns,* no, nothing like that back home.

"Not like here. Here, I worry for you, Laura. *Grauslige* men are everywhere, just waiting for a chance at you. Every time you go out, I worry that something will happen."

"Oma, I can take care of myself," I say.

"No," Oma replies, "you can never know. When they want it…" She looks at me so solemnly that I have to look away.

OMA AND MY ONKEL FRANK are sitting at the heavy oak table after supper, reminiscing as usual. The first day of our visit was bright and cloudless after the night rain, but the autumn warmth has vanished with the sun. Now there is only candlelight, and thick northern darkness outside the cottage window. Crystal glasses, red wine. Tante Frances is washing dishes. I am drying them carefully, putting them away.

"We were sitting outside the cellar bunker," Frank is saying, "when it went through the brick wall, left just a little hole like this in the brick wall, and exploded inside. Made such a mess…smoked strings of sausages, hams, jars of preserves, wine bottles went flying everywhere." Frank's hands are demonstrating the explosion. I wonder when he will knock his glass over. "The walls, everything was stained and dripping with dark red wine and beet juice. It was that close." He shakes his head. Takes a slow sip of wine.

"Where was this?" I ask, turning from the sink with the plate I am wiping.

"This was the first place we fled to in the forest behind the village, in the mountains. The place those women died, you've probably heard that part."

"No."

"The mother who went mad, and her two girls," says Oma. "On the day before the Russians came."

"What?" I put the plate down on the counter. "How old were these girls?"

Frank looks at me, tilts his head slightly. "Your age."

"No, fifteen and seventeen," Oma says.

I take the dish towel and try to focus on wiping and stacking.

"Oma, do I know this story?"

"No," Oma says with quiet finality. But Frank pushes his chair back from the table in a screech of wood on wood, and turns to face me squarely.

"You want the story? Here's the story." He gulps some wine.

"Before the Russians came, they turned the night into day. So many *Raketen*—missiles, they were firing so many *Raketen,* that the sky was a bright orange green in the middle of the night. We were all nervous, wondering if they would find us.

"That woman, though, she got a little nuts. That's when she found—I'll never forget it—that little trophy I won at the *Hitlerjugend* games I told you about. For running fast I won it. Anyways, her eyes went real wide, really wide open, and she took it outside, and got a hammer and started hammering and hammering this thing until it was flat. She thought that when the Russians came and found it they would rape her and kill her. She took it and threw it into the *Guelle,* the liquid manure, so they wouldn't find it for sure. And her girls, she went on and on about how she would hide them from the Russians, how they wouldn't get her girls. We had a few bottles of wine left, too, that she dumped on the dung heap so the Russians wouldn't drink it. Then the chickens, the chickens got all drunk and started wobbling and flapping and falling all over the place." Frank is chuckling softly, and I can hear the squawking, can see clumps of little feathered bodies tumbling down the dung heap.

"So anyways, she was going on like this all night..." His voice dies.

"We went to bed," continues Oma. "No one thought to watch her." She shakes her head, stares down into her wine. Then she looks at me. "Such beautiful children, tall and smart. Long, thick hair they had, and so clever." She holds my gaze.

"And?" I hear myself say.

"And she coaxed the girls up into the hay loft and—"

"Well anyways, to make this shorter," Frank interrupts. He is shifting in his chair, twirling his wine glass, empty again, back and forth between his fingers. "I went into the barn and saw them hanging there. I thought at first that they were dolls. Ghosts in women's dresses, hovering in there above the hay..."

"Frank cut them down," says Oma.

"I went up there and cut them down, all three. First she hanged the girls, then herself." Frank spreads his strong, skilled hands, closes his fists, grasping air. "I thought I could save them ... I just climbed up there and cut them all down... without thinking. As if any twelve-year-old boy could think. But the girls were already dead. She wasn't, though, the mother lived another day. Just lay there in the hay convulsing." He turns to Oma. "What was it she kept saying?"

"She was calling their names," Oma says quietly, "Maria and Theresa. I remember. Someone fetched the doctor, but he couldn't help her. The next day the Russians came. They asked what was the matter with her. Someone explained that she hanged her children and herself, and they turned their heads away."

"Of course, if the Russians had caught them, those girls, they would have raped them," Frank says thoughtfully, "they raped all the girls."

"Yes," Oma says." Everyone but the mothers with babies. Your mother, she saved me."

"So she killed her children," I say. "I don't understand. Why didn't they try to get away? Surely they could have saved themselves."

"*Ha*, she convinced them somehow," says Oma, lifting her shoulders. "She was their mother. She wanted to save them. She convinced them that she knew best, and that it was better for them to die."

She falls silent as Frank pours more wine. Tante Frances is still washing at the sink behind me. Her face is set; has she been listening at all? The water runs, stops. Dishes are piling up in my dish rack.

"*Ja*," Oma says, "she loved them. She loved them that much."

The Russians

*T*HE NIGHT COLD HAS SEEPED IN through cracks in the door, and the candles on the table are flickering. I feel familiar ghosts hovering just beyond the circles of light. Oma shivers, and I bring a woolly blanket to cover her knees. Onkel Frank has gone out behind the cabin to bring in more wood for the fire. Tante Frances and I finish up in the kitchen, and we join Oma at the table. She pours us each another glass of wine.

"*Ja,*" Oma says, "when the Russians came, we were all in the bunker, in the forest, in the mountains, the whole town. We thought the Russians wouldn't go there. But they got there even before they reached the village. It was a beautiful, clear day, I remember so well. Bright sky, green everywhere. The first day in spring when I didn't have my wool stockings on. I was walking with your mother, had her in my arms, *nit,* when one of them came riding up to me from out of the woods. A nice horse, he had, big and black and snorting. The baby had a cold, and I was wiping her nose with a blue handkerchief, the ones us farmers had. He stopped right in front of us and watched me, his horse dancing and snorting at us. Then he jumped off his horse and ripped the handkerchief from my hand. He ripped it out of my hand and threw it away.

"I didn't dare say anything, I couldn't speak. He narrowed his eyes and looked at me. Big dark eyes he had, and thick eyebrows. '*Hat er gsog.* Not good! *Hat er gsog,* baby, *hat er gsog, muss a weisses hoam.*' He reached into his cape like he was angry and I thought he was reaching for a gun. But he pulled out three clean, white handkerchiefs and gave them to me. For the baby. The blue one he wouldn't let me collect, I had to leave it."

The door of the cabin swings open, and Frank shoulders his way in, his arms laden with wood.

"*Ja,* the Russians loved children. *Gell,* right, Frank, they loved children."

Frank nods as he feeds the fire.

"And mothers," Oma continues. "If you had a baby they left you alone. 'You mama, you mama?' they would say, and smile at Erika. But those who had no babies with them, they took them out of the bunker, and raped them."

"Oma, how many Russians came?" I ask.

"How many? I don't know. They came like bees, more than you could count. I can't tell you how many. The German troops tried to stop them but they just kept coming and coming, pushing those Germans back.

"We were staying with the Schrebers in the forest. I was careful to have your mother with me all the time, but the Schreber girl, they took her out of their house, to the big *Misthaufen.* They threw her onto this dung heap, and the Russians lined up. One off her, the next on, eight or nine at a time.

"They all had the *Geschlechtskrankheit,* the *Sibillia,* they called it."

"Syphilis?"

"*Ja, sauwos.* The girls and women who were raped had to go every day to the midwife, and she burned them out. With a hot iron rod. Burned the sickness out.

"I held her hand, the Schreber girl, because her mother couldn't do it. Her fingernails would break my skin, make me bleed. She had it really bad, the sickness, but she didn't die until later, after we were deported. There was nothing left of her, all sunken in, the flesh hanging away from her bones. Such a beautiful girl. She lived and lived, but her eyes were empty. And finally, when we were deported on the transport train, she died."

I pretend that I have to use the bathroom, and stumble away from the table. I sink to the cool, tile floor with the lights off, and press my fingers into my temples. I should just go to bed, I think, it's late.

"I can still remember word for word what she said," Frank is saying when I return to them. He takes one of the wine bottles and drains the last drops into his glass. The bottle leaves rings of red on the table where it stood. The candles have burned to stumps of glistening wax. Frank is laughing silently, his chest heaving. "She sat down in the kitchen and said now I've had enough for my whole life."

"What?"

"She was a woman no one would have," explains Oma, "and she thought now's a time I can get enough, and they took her over and over." Their laughter is jagged, almost painful, smothering the words. "And after the first time she came back, she came back and said now I have had enough. Five or six were on her at once, like bees, stinging, and she comes back and can hardly walk, and says 'It burns like hell, I've had enough now.,"

Oma can barely bring the words out she is laughing so hard. The hysteria is infectious; I am laughing now too. I don't know why. Laughter without mirth. Tears run down Frank's face.

"One time," he says, "one time she said, one wanted me, and I farted...and then she would fart every time one wanted to do her, and they would kick her and say '*Du Schwein.*' But they left her alone."

We are laughing and crying. The candle flames catch our breath and cast erratic shadows on the curtains. There is a rushing in my ears, I feel the pulse at my temples, and I think if I stop laughing I will explode.

Frank blurts, "'I can fart when I want,' she said."

Oma has tears running into her mouth. "Oh, God, *na.*"

I WAKE TO THE SOUND OF COFFEE percolating mixed with the undulating tones of voices. Sunlight is filtering through the fir trees outside, casting mottled patterns across the bedspread. Shoving the hair from my eyes, I stumble out to the kitchen. I wonder if I am the only one whose head is still throbbing. Oma and Frank fall silent as I join them at the table. Tante Frances slides a coffee mug into my hands.

"Sleep well?" Frank asks. I grin crookedly, and nod.

Frank and Oma exchange a look. There is a curious silence.

"Laura, what we talked about last night...you aren't going to use that in your stories, are you?" Frank asks. "I mean, it's not a good story, you know?" I blow the steam off my mug and think. I have never seen him embarrassed before. Oma stays silent.

It is Frances who says, "No, Frank. Let her decide. It is all part of the story, all of it." I look up at my aunt in surprise, thankful for this unexpected offering. She puts her hands on her husband's shoulders, and he sighs. Later she will pull me aside and say, "Laura, it is good what you are doing. They both need you to listen."

I turn to Oma. "So...what happened next?"

"Next? *Ha,* I don't know where we stopped," she says, her mouth full of buttered toast.

"You were in the bunker," Frances prompts.

"Oh, *ja.* And then the Germans pushed the Russians back, in the night. We were all still in the bunker. And then the Germans came over the loudspeaker and told us all to flee, to leave everything and flee, because if the Russians returned they would kill us all. So we all fled, as we were, toward Burgenland province in Austria. Before we got to the border, there the Russians were standing. And when we wanted to come out of the forest, they saw us and started shooting. They had a gun set up with thirty, forty shots in it, duit duit duit duit," she jabs with her finger, "they mowed you down."

Frank joins in. "First there was a ditch that the panzer tanks couldn't go through," he explains, "then a minefield, then the wire that they opened up so we could go through."

"Erika I had in my arms," says Oma, "and Rudi on my back, because with his bad foot he could hardly walk, and Frank beside me carried two bags. And I tried to run like that."

"We just got out of the forest, and in front of us was open field. And there were the Russians still, we could hear them, and they were bombarding. The Germans yelled 'Go back! Go back!' So we left the suitcases and ran like hell back into the forest."

"Wait," I say, "I'm confused. Where were the Russians?"

"They were in front of us, at the border," Frank tries to explain, "and more were coming from behind us somewhere."

"We all went back," says Oma, "and one soldier, a German soldier, slipped secretly in after us to lead us safely out of the forest, where the Russians wouldn't see us. He took Erika and Rudi in his arms, and led us through that hell. There was a forest path that led all the way to the Burgenland side. So many dead ones were lying in there, Russians. Do you remember, Frank?"

"Oh, *ja*, I remember, all right. We had to step over them."

"It's not good to think about it." Oma shivers.

"When we were over the border," she continues, "that soldier took me into a house, and got the woman there to give us something to eat, and then he disappeared. I never got to thank him or anything."

"He was probably killed that day," Frank says.

"*Ja*, so many died in that place. So many."

The toaster pops with a twang of metal springs, and I place a slice onto Oma's plate.

"Then I went to Langzeil, over by Güssing," Oma says, "to my Aunt Resi's, with Rudi and Erika and Frank. There it was better. We didn't have to be so afraid. A week the Germans held the front. But the Russians, they finally broke through. So many Russians came that they just couldn't hold them off. And so we stayed with Tante Resi until the war was really over. The Russians came there too, but they left us alone mostly. Resi had four or five children, and I had three, *nit*.

"We stayed two or three weeks more. When they were hungry, the Russians, they shot up chickens, and brought them to Resi's to cook. They made a stew with potatoes and chicken and everything they could find. And it was good. You just had to watch your teeth on the lead from the bullets they sprayed at the chickens, *nit*. Whatever they had left over they gave us. Gave the children, mostly, *nit*, because they liked the children so much. And they had lots of cattle in the meadows, that they'd stolen and driven with them, and the women had to milk them, and got milk for the children, and for ourselves.

"There was one Russian who worked the telephones, a young *Kerl* who came every day and brought me a loaf of bread. For the children. He could speak a little bit of German. He always sat down by me, and wouldn't let me go milk the cows because I had a baby. He sat by me and said mama, mama, *du* come in Russland. He said when he goes back to Russia, I have to go with him. There, the women are not allowed to work, he said, there, I would have it good. He was very earnest about this. As I said, he brought me bread, every day. A big loaf."

I wonder what became of that young soldier, what he found when or if he returned to Mother Russia. I see a vast ocean of communist-style wheat fields spanning the centrefold of a *National Geographic,* and images of the army of bent-backed, leather-skinned women working those fields.

I think of the loaves of dark rye my mother buys at Dimpfelmeiers in Toronto. They are almost three feet long, with a deep brown, floured crust. We slice it into chunks and freeze it. I usually bring a loaf when we go up north to visit. There is a picture of Onkel Frank hefting one of those loaves in his hands the way he would a prize fish.

"And then one day," Oma continues, "the children, the baby, too, were with Tante Resi somewhere, I don't know anymore why, and I got home, alone, to Resi's house. I went in, and something felt wrong, I don't know how. And then I went into the bedroom, and there was a Russian inside. In the bedroom. Standing by the bed with his face to the wall. He turned when he heard me, and I wanted to run away. But he said 'No mama, no mama, *komm her, komm her,*' he said, 'come here.' And he wasn't coming at me or anything. Just staying in the corner and motioning with his hand that I should come to him. I didn't move. And you know what he did then? He turned back to the wall." Oma takes a slow slurp of coffee.

"*Ja.* And then I saw where he was looking. We had pictures of Jesus and Maria on the wall. I took a step into the room. I could see then that he was standing in front of those pictures, and he was praying. I went closer, and looked with him at the Christ and His mother, and I saw how sad they looked. The soldier turned to me. 'Ruskie,' he said to me, 'we also have Jesus *und* Maria.' He was already an older man, with thick, creased skin. A farmer's skin, like my husband. I sat beside him on the bed, and he talked and talked, but I didn't understand the Russian, of course. Then he stood up and crossed himself to Maria. 'Thank you,' he said to me, 'thank you.' He came often after that. Always to pray by the pictures."

With a clatter of plates and cutlery, we clear the table.

"And then the war was over," Oma says. "The Russians came in the morning and danced and sang in the rain, and shot in the air. 'Hitler *kaput,* Hitler *kaput,*' they sang, 'Hitler *kaput!*' And they threw money around, and the children gathered it up."

Potato Dynamics

"WHEN IT WAS SAFE AGAIN," Oma says, "after the front moved through Jakobshof, nit, I took your mother and went down from the mountain to see how it was at home. I had to go through the forest. There were Russians everywhere, with their horses and cannons. But they didn't do anything to me, because I had a baby. It must have been mid-summer, but it was cold. Cold enough to wear gloves and wool stockings. I remember because mine were sagging, they were so stretched out, but I was afraid to pull them up with those soldiers leering."

The afternoon sky has darkened. Oma turns the kitchen light on. We are wrapping small, blue-purple plums in squares of potato dough for *Zwetschgenknödel.*

"*Ja,* it was cold. Maybe that's why the corpses in the forest didn't smell too much. There was so much rotting fruit everywhere, since no one harvested the early crop. I do remember that it stunk. *Pfui,* it stunk so rotten-sweet. But I felt so sorry for those dead soldiers, Germans they were. One, I can still see him, he was sitting with his back against a tree, with a hole in his stomach. Still had a piece of bread in his hand."

Suddenly my fingers feel sticky. I look down and realize I have punctured the plum cupped in my palm. Plum juice oozes from the indentations my fingernails have made.

"And so I got to the village. The only light was at the school. I went in, and they stopped talking and glared at me. They were all there, all the ones who were still at home, the older men and some women, having a meeting. The *Richter,* he was there, and the mayor. They were important men now, so half-communist, *nit,* in with the

Russians. My sister-in-law who had lived with us, Celi, she was there, too. I hardly recognized her, she was so thin, and so ragged-looking. I went to stand by her but she looked so sour, I thought she was going to spit on me."

The community was tiny. Fifteen houses, maybe. Before the war, everyone in that room must have been a friend, a neighbour, a relative. These stories are so hard to understand.

"Then the mayor," Oma continues, "he said to me, '*Na*,' says he, '*Laura, du hast nichts mehr.* Your land has been divided and you have nothing'. And I said, 'how come?' '*Ja*,' he says, 'those who had nothing got, and those who had something, everything was taken from them.' And then I said, 'OK, all right,' I said."

"What? Oma, how could they do that?"

"*Ha, es woar Krieg.* It was war. What could I do about it? They did what they wanted."

"But why did you let them?" I say, my voice rising.

"Laura, have you even ever seen a gun?" Oma says.

I think a minute. Shake my head.

"But weren't you mad?" I ask quietly.

"Oh, *ja*, I was mad. Of course I was. But what could I do? Your grandfather, he was in Gmunden, *nit*, in the prisoner camp. I was alone.

"And our mayor, he turned to my sister-in-law and said the same thing. 'You have nothing, all has been taken, because *der Franzl*—my husband—had everything'."

What a convenient interpretation of communism. And Franz, my Opa, did they conveniently forget him? Probably figured that any man not present was dead, anyways. The convenience of those passive words: All has been taken. As though it were not completely their doing, as though it were out of their control.

"And Celi started to argue with them, but they just looked at her. Stupid. So I said, 'OK, *nehmts oalles, fraissts oalles, hani gsog, und mochts wos wults, hani gsog*,' and then I went to leave."

It's completely amazing that Oma's dramatic spirit didn't get her killed. I can see her standing with my mother tightly in her arms, sagging stockings and wild dark hair. I see her flinging the words into their thieving faces. 'Take everything, eat everything, and do what you like!' The fierceness of these words is dulled by their English translation.

"So I went to leave, but the mayor, he blocked the door. He was a big man, with a thick, black beard, and such a stomach you have never seen. He stood over me, and said, 'You shut up with your big mouth,' he said, 'we'll put you out in the forest,' he said, 'and you can look in from there.'

"There was spit flying out of his mouth. I felt it hit my cheek. I stood right close and looked up and said, *'von mir aus, hani gsog,* put me out there, take my children,' I said, 'and eat them.'

"He was breathing down on me, hard, full of garlic, and I thought he was going to blow up right in front of me. But then he stopped. He stopped, and looked at his shoes. All of a sudden, it was so quiet. I looked around the room, but nobody would look back at me, nobody. I went out the door and away."

"They were ashamed, weren't they Oma?"

"*Ha,* maybe. Maybe."

THE LITTLE GIRL IS STANDING on a chair beside Oma at the counter. "*Zucker brauch mir jetzt,*" Oma says, and the little girl jumps off the chair and fetches the sugar tin. She is having a cooking lesson, Oma-style. The other ingredients are lined up on the counter, casting shadows on the wall like a skyline. Flour for bulk, she learns. Eggs to make things stick. Salt, of course. Always *eine Prise.* A pinch.

Oma reaches for the milk carton, tearing a skyscraper from the shadow city. In the mixing bowl are boiled potatoes that the little girl has mashed with a big fork. Oma adds milk while her granddaughter stirs. Then Oma pours sugar into her palm. The crystals are bright against the thick, waxy skin. Those hands can plunge into boiling water and barely feel a thing.

"Give me your hand," Oma says, and transfers the sugar into the smaller palm until it is full. "This much," she says.

Five boiled potatoes make approximately twenty Zwetschgenknöedel, *so you'll need twenty plums. This is the only measurement I can write down for you, Mom. It depends how big the potatoes are, and how thin you roll out the dough…I'm skipping ahead, sorry. How can I describe the "dollop" of milk Oma adds? And the flour, you add flour to the mixture until, well, until it doesn't need any more. Don't forget the pinch of salt. This isn't helping you much, is it?*

It's the potatoes you are craving again, I'm sure. I never thought you'd ask me for cooking advice. You hate cooking, you've always said so.

"SO I WENT TO OUR HOUSE," Oma continues. We are boiling the *Knödel* now, in the massive steel pot. When they rise to the surface, white and puffy, I transfer them to the pan of fried breadcrumbs and sugar. Oma rolls them around until they are coated.

"Celi followed me," she says, "yelling the whole time. At me, at everything. The whole village felt strange, like an empty husk. And when I saw the house, I stopped. Celi shut up.

"The Germans, when they retreated, they blew up their panzers so the Russians wouldn't have them. They blew one up right outside our gate. Part of it was stuck in the roof — there was a big hole. And all the windows were shattered, except the kitchen window, I don't know why. All the windows were stuffed with newspapers and straw. The door was open, swinging on one hinge. I didn't want to touch anything."

I see the house, the doorway. A dark, gaping wound in the wall. I don't want her to go in.

"So we went in," Oma continues. "It was dim, because of the blocked windows, but when we could see, there was nothing there. Everything was gone, even the beds. The floors in all the rooms were covered with dirty straw. Russians slept there. *Und es hat so gestunken,* so badly it stank, of piss and of alcohol.

"Then Celi came alive again, and started going through the rooms, shouting again. She found a broom, the broom he made, my husband, and the baskets he wove, and everything she could find she took. She had no more claim than I, but I said take it, you can have it all, I need nothing. The kitchen was bare, but there were chicken feathers sticking in blood on the sink basin, and down the cupboard. The Russians, they must have cooked. I had no dishes to cook with, nothing, *nit*, everything was gone.

"And when I went into the yard to look, I had no lard, the lard I had buried and the flour were gone. The neighbour had dug it up. Celi left then, I'm not sure where she went. And I went down into the root cellar. It was damp and dark without a light. But I could see that everything from there was gone, too. But in the corner, in a trough, were potatoes. Not this year's crop, but old and shrivelled. And for that year, '45, from those potatoes we lived…potatoes every day."

When the potatoes bloom, you tell me, they are beautiful. Whole fields of delicate flowers. A sea of green, studded with tiny white stars. There were fields outside the barracks where you lived in Germany after they deported you, after the war, weren't there? Those decrepit barracks where you Flüchtlinge were forced to live have long since been torn down, erased from the gently rolling landscape.

You didn't see much of Oma in those years when you were little, did you? She rose early and headed to the fields, or went to clean the homes of townspeople who paid her in sacks of flour. Did you know that the food she brought home for you, Rudi and Frank in the evening was the lunch she earned and didn't eat?

You all helped with the potatoes, you tell me. Squatting among the plants, it was your job to pick off the potato bugs. You shudder as insect feet scuttle grotesquely across your memory. They were big, these beetles, as big as a quarter, with a hard shell. Holding one between thumb and forefinger, you searched for a stone to crush it against with your heel. From across the rows where Oma was working, the sickening crunch crunch made you wince. She was squishing them in her hands, beetle guts oozing from between her fingers.

Oma tried to show you how, didn't she, but you would have none of it. I see you, wispy blond hair clipped neatly in barrettes at your temples, scrunching up your face in disgust, looking at Oma, sensing already then that you were different.

THE LITTLE GIRL DRAGS THE CHAIR across the linoleum to the sink. From the chair she can reach down into the big red mixing bowl. She plunges both hands into the soft potato mixture. They get stuck. A strand of hair falls across her face, and she tries to blow it away.

This memory smells of hot potatoes, but only faintly. I didn't know there were any in the dough until I learned to make it; you can't taste them.

Oma pushes her granddaughter's sleeves up past her elbows. When the girl manages to extract her hands, they are webbed with dough. She dreams that night of swimming like a duck.

"Like this," Oma says. Taking one of her granddaughter's hands into her own, she begins to knead with a rhythm as natural to those fingers as the flowing of blood through their veins. Round and round the flour-lined bowl the dough is pushed and pulled, pushed and pulled by those skilled hands. The movement is strong, fluid, sensual.

"Don't be afraid of the dough," she says as the little girl tries to copy. "Let the fingers learn the rhythm."

Together they roll out the dough until it covers the whole countertop. Then Oma slices the sheet into squares, and the little girl carefully places the plums on them. "When your mother was your age," Oma says, "she used to swallow the plum stones so that no one could tell how many *Zwetschgenknödeln* she'd eaten."

I have a hazy memory of being in Oma's room, of seeing her in bed and you holding a steaming pot over her, tilting it so the contents slosh to the edge...I smell ferns.

Now I remember. She had a bad back for a while. I wasn't in school yet. Those were the frightening days of your collaborative cooking attempts.

You made a lot of potato meals when Oma was sick. I remember, because I still hated them then. Except for French fries, of course. When Oma was healthy and you were at work, Oma would call me to her and whisper, Let's go to McDonald's, but don't tell your mother. Our secret. Why it was a secret, I'm not sure. Now you know.

When Oma was sick, I tried to be good and stay out of the way, especially in the kitchen. The pot you are holding in my memory smells of Krumpenkauch—potato chunks and spicy sausage in a thick sauce—the peasant's specialty.

I remember listening to you banging around the kitchen searching for ingredients, muttering to yourself. I sat on the floor by the fridge, wanting to help, wanting to be invisible. You hesitated with the paprika powder or pepper shaker in your hand. *How much? How much?* You reached for the measuring cups and spoons, the implements of your careful cooking style, but for this Oma-recipe, they were of no use. You glared into the pot in frustration. The steam curling up from it made your hair droop flat against your face, for once inelegant. And then you grabbed the pot and I followed you up to Oma's room.

She couldn't sit up in bed, or even turn her head, but you needed her to see. So you tilted the pot as far as you dared. Another inch and Oma would have had a boiling hot potato mixture in her lap. Oma shifted a little, making the pillowcases full of dried ferns rustle beneath her. They are her remedy for all aches and pains. *Please let her get well soon,* I prayed to those ferns.

"The consistency is wrong," Oma said, catching a glimpse of the mashed Krumpenkauch. And, with a wrinkle of her nose, "Why haven't you put in more paprika." A command, not a question.

Down to the kitchen you went. Muttered, banged around some more. Repeated your trip upstairs.

Eventually we would eat. I dreaded those meals. My stomach invariably gurgled and ached for hours afterwards, but I never let on.

THE WARM YELLOW LIGHT FROM THE STOVE falls on the three figures at the table. That the two younger women are related, there is no doubt. Strangers — all men — have stopped them in the street to comment on the resemblance. "You two must be sisters," they say slyly. The mother smiles. Her daughter does not. So we have the same nose, she thinks, the same hair, so what? Don't they notice that I am three inches taller, that she could fit her slender form inside of mine with room to spare? They can't resist her; men are attracted like moths to a light. And I can't even get a date.

The girl is eighteen; beyond the house, she is a woman. Not bad looking. Not her mother's size four, but fit.

Oma sits closest to the stove. What does she see when she looks at her daughter and granddaughter?

The pan full of golden *Zwetschgenknödel* is still on the stove. As many are left over as they have just eaten. There is never too little to eat in Oma's kitchen.

Oma goes to spoon another *Knödel* onto her granddaughter's plate.

"*Komm, iss na iss, eat eat, du hast ja goar nichts gessen.*"

"I have *too* eaten," says the girl, covering her plate with her hand, "and I'm done for now, thanks, Oma. They were really good." Her plate is lined with plum pits, like so many shiny purple beetles.

"But there are still so many on the stove, eat, or they will all be leftovers," entreats Oma, the *Knödel* still on the spoon. "You know if we don't clear our plates it will rain tomorrow."

The girl's mother shifts in her chair.

"That's a silly myth," says the girl, "and the garden is dry."

"I think she's had enough," says her mother to Oma. They exchange a look. Oma's eyes narrow with disapproval. Mother sets her jaw.

"Why do you always have to speak for me? I'm eighteen years old, I can say no for myself," says the girl, dismayed. Here we go again, she thinks.

"Oh can you? Then why don't you?" her mother says.

"I just did!"

They glare at each other. The girl is being drawn in even though she has vowed to stop letting them get to her.

"Look at Oma's face," says her mother, "she doesn't believe you." Oma is sitting now with her hands in her lap. The look on her face is a mix of disapproval and resignation. She looks old.

"OK, fine," says the girl. "Fine. Oma, I'm finished, I'm full. I'm stuffed."

Oma looks at her granddaughter, a quizzical smile lifting her features. She sighs with her whole body.

"There, look at that, she thinks it's all my fault. Everything's always my fault," the girl's mother says. She punctuates her statements with a stab of her fork.

The girl looks at her blankly. "What are you talking about?"

"You aren't eating more because I don't want you to, isn't that right, Oma? You think I haven't raised her properly. You think I'm trying to starve her, to put her on a diet, right?"

Oma just looks at her. Sighs again.

"What's your fault?" the girl asks.

Her mother ignores her. "Or do you think she's afraid to take more," she continues, "afraid there isn't enough? This isn't a war!"

The girl takes a deep breath. Closes her eyes so she won't roll them and make things worse.

"So what do you want me to do, tell her again?" she says evenly.

"Yes!"

"Oma," the girl says, letting her voice rise, "Oma, I'm so full I'm going to be sick if I eat another bite, do you want me to be sick?"

Oma raises her eyebrows, but stays silent. The girl grabs the plates and stacks them with a clatter.

"You two are unbelievable!" she says on her way to the sink. She dumps the plates, stomps out of the kitchen. Storms up the stairs.

In the stillness of her mother's closet, she lets herself sink to the floor, exhausted. The girl has inherited the family flare for the dramatic, but she is drained by the performance.

She closes her eyes and breathes in the mother-smell in the hanging clothes. But this is not a refuge. She reaches behind the shoes for the chocolate stash, kept there because the closet is cold. It is not off limits, but her mother would disapprove, she is sure. Her body is tense again, every sense straining for the sound of footsteps on the stairs, in the hall. The adrenaline makes her feel sick, even as she unwraps the bar of rich Austrian chocolate. She carefully arranges the remaining bars so this one won't be missed. Stuffs the wrapper into her pocket. Later she will carefully hide it beneath other garbage. Very deliberate; she leaves no trace.

The girl inhales that chocolate, barely chewing. Doesn't enjoy it. No. Hardly even tastes it.

Marriage

*T*WO PHOTOS HAVE SURVIVED from Oma's wedding. One is a group shot, the other a photo of the bride and groom standing against the wall of the sturdy, weathered wooden barn. Opa is in a dark suit. Oma is in a simple white dress. The material of a sheer veil falls past her shoulders from a circlet of lace held in place on her head with delicate wire clips. Opa's bright eyes are overexposed, making him look haunted. Oma's pretty, young face is set, grim. Her eyes, staring hard into the camera, are solemn. The impression the newlyweds leave on film is not one of a couple facing a promising future together. Side by side, not touching, unsmiling they stare into the camera. I think of a mug shot.

"Oma, why don't you and Opa look happy?" I asked her once.

"Oh," said Oma, running her fingers along the raised edge of the photograph, "that's because it was taken a week after the wedding. The photographer, he was always drunk, so he didn't show up for the real day.

"The weather turned humid in the week after the wedding, really stiflingly. We had just come in from the fields all dirty and hot when he showed up with his bad teeth and greasy head and said, 'Let's do the wedding picture.' I started to say no, but my new husband turned to me and said, '*Kiem na,* Laura, come on, let's just do it.' So I put my wedding dress back on, on my smelly, sticky body, and my sister Resi clipped the veil into my hair. The photographer placed us against the barn and started setting up his camera. I stood there and focused on two manure flies circling his head. I watched them take turns landing on his hair, his ears, his nose. I stood there watching those two flies dance and prayed that Franz wouldn't put his arm around me, that he wouldn't touch me. In that *grauslige* heat I could feel a fat bead of sweat trickling slowly down between my shoulder blades. The thought of a moist hand against my back, against my skin, made me nauseous.

"For the group shot we gathered as much of the wedding party together as we could, but some people were not home. That's why Eddi Schreiver is in the picture and not Josef Schrei. That's why I look so mad."

I am in Oma's room, helping her slip a fresh cover onto the mattress, helping work the bulky softness of her *Federbett* into its soft pastel case. We pick up the corners of the duvet and shake it, so that the feathers even out inside. When I was little, Oma would tell the story of Frau Holle, the old woman who lives in the sky. When this woman takes her *Federbett* to the window and shakes and shakes it, somewhere in the world it snows.

When we are done, I straighten the portrait of my Opa hanging above the bed.

"You know," Oma says, "I married him when I was eighteen." She is sitting on the freshly made bed, absently picking bits of down from her clothes.

"When did you meet my Opa?" I ask, sinking down beside her.

"My husband? I don't even know. Whenever they needed people to work on the farm, my mother would work for them, my husband's people. If we ever needed anything done he always came over and did it, my husband, as a boy. He was ten years older than me. I never dreamed we would marry. He was always at our place, fixing things, doing what work we could not do without horses. They had horses, but we had only two cows.

"He arranged with my mother that he would marry me, you know. Already when I was sixteen they arranged this, but no one told me."

"What do you mean you didn't know?" I ask.

"*Ha,*" she says, shrugging, "*es woar holt sau.* Nobody told me. And I went everywhere with him because I was not afraid of him, was not afraid he would do anything to me. No, not him. When there was music somewhere we would go together, and when I saw that another one wanted to go home with me, one I didn't trust, I always said, 'Binder, aren't you going home yet?' *'Ja,'* he grumbled, *'heit bin i wider guit* — for today I am good enough — *gell, hat er gsog, gell?'* And often I went home with him like that. I didn't think anything of it then. *I konnte ihn guit leiden, nit,* and so it went."

I konnte ihn guit leiden. I liked him a lot, she means. At least, I think so. Literally translated, it means that she could suffer him well. *Leiden* is to suffer or endure, but *Leidenschaft* is the word for passion.

"What was Opa like?" I ask.

"What was he like? Like he is here in this photo." She points to the poorly touched-up photo on the wall.

"No, Oma, what was his personality like?"

She looks puzzled, unsure of what I am asking. "What do you mean? With me? He could dance well, and he was friendly and danced with everyone too, no one was not good enough. Some of the farmers thought themselves better than the rest of us, but he, the richest one of them all, he wasn't like that." There is a pride in her voice, and warmth, the same warmth with which she speaks of wine making and of harvest feasts.

"And then I liked him, and we came to be together. I was eighteen."

"So young, Oma," I say softly.

She sighs and folds her hands in her lap. Looks at me with a weary grin and says, "*Ja,* I was. Most of us were. *Ja, i han holt goar nit gwisst.* I didn't know anything about anything — *i hamma denkt, hairat holt, nit, bin i a dumm gwesen, nit,* I didn't know what difference marriage would make. Was I dumb. He always said, '*Ja,* we have to marry, we have to marry.' And so we married."

"Were you in love with him?"

"What?"

"Oma, did you love him?"

"Love? Well, yes. Of course." She unfolds a pillowcase, shakes it open. "I trusted him. *I konnte ihn guit leiden, nit.*"

Thirty days he gave you to decide. Totally unexpected, the ring, the proposal. You were surprised, dizzy with your perfume and his smell and your uncertainty. Sitting on his lap, his dark eyes close, full of gentle but insistent question marks. Wanting to spin away, twirl out of his arms.

Wanting to melt into them, into love. Ich bin in ihm verliebt: In German you are not in love with *him, but in love* in *him; a difference.*

After six months, how well can you know someone? Till death do us part sounds like such a very long time. You laugh now at the memory. Thirty days. Thirty day return policy on the ring.

You met in the sky. I love this story. Thirty-four thousand feet over the outer Hebrides, your colleague Sylvie sends you up to the cockpit to check out the really cute first officer—for her, of course. Soft curves and clean edges cutting a stunning figure in your Air Canada uniform, you go up front to ask if the pilots want more coffee.

His name is John Taylor. Of course he falls for you, and you for him. Or at least that's how the story goes. Love above the clouds.

Wait, it gets better. You land in Paris. It is February, but it is mild and you walk and walk together, drunk with lack of sleep and time change. You drift into a cafe in Montmartre, in the shadow of Sacre Coeur. Saying little, you take turns reading each other's faces—the soft line of a cheek-bone, whisper of an eyebrow. You are lovers with your eyes long before even your fingers touch.

Rushing out of your room for crew pick-up the next morning, you almost crush it with your suitcase. The rose on the floor with the note—"Je t'aime." Ich liebe dich. The same as I love you? A beginning.

'Wow,' you say after I read this section to you over the phone, 'that was us. Beautiful—you got it just right—I have to cry. It's all true. Except, well, it was November, not February, and we had to sit inside because it started to rain. And it was Zurich we first landed in. Haven't I ever shown you the photos?'

"SO TELL ME about your wedding, Oma."

We are still sitting on Oma's bed, our bodies pressing down into the fluffy *Federbett*. I pull my knees in to my chest, leaving ravines in the fabric landscape where my legs have been. The cover is still warm from the dryer, and the air in the room is thick with a fresh laundry smell and with Oma's words.

"The wedding? My husband's people drove us to the church in their carriage, all covered with flowers. Even the manes and tails of the horses had flowers braided in. The church was far into the forest. Everything was green, green. Wait…the eighteenth of May it was, I think.

"After the church we ate and drank and danced. It was in the house you saw, my mother's house. About sixty people came, and we spent the whole night eating and drinking and dancing.

"First we had a soup, a good soup with *Knödel*. Then we had chicken, cooked and baked chicken, and juicy *Schnitzel,* and pork, and smoked meat, and ham with bread and sauce and cabbage and potatoes. And after there was *Kuchen* of course, all kinds…Until midnight we ate."

I have to smile. I know she could elaborate on this menu endlessly even if she were to forget everything else.

"Then we began to dance. First was the *Ehrentanz.* All the men there had to dance with the bride. And they had to pay. The money collected went to the musicians. They could toss as much into the pot as they wanted. '*Ich bin gereist über die Wiener strossen, Silber und Gold hat mich verlossen, Silber und Gold er glänzt so schen, der und der muss tanzen gehen'*." (Eeny meeny miney mo.) She half sings the nonsense rhyme, pointing her finger at the men lining the dance floor of her memory.

"And then you danced with Opa?"

"Oh, *ja,* he was a good dancer. I'm sure we danced. Later I had to sit down in the middle of the dance floor and they took off my wreath and veil, and they played another game with me…I don't remember what."

"But Oma, what about your husband, didn't you celebrate together?" I am waiting to see the passionate kiss, to hear people clapping and laughing and admiring the happy couple.

"*Ja,* he was there too, of course. Then I changed into other clothes and the celebration continued until the sun came up. We didn't have a honeymoon, or sleep together or anything. He went home and I lay down for a while, but I didn't sleep. Everything had to be cleaned up, *nit*. And then it was time to go to work."

He would always run a bath for you when you came home from a flight. My dad, that is. John would run you a bath, and then he would sit on a chair beside the tub for your "debriefing." You would soak your tired body under the bubbles and tell him of the places you'd been, the difficult people you'd encountered, of the lonely hotel room. The stressful work of walking across the Atlantic would evaporate in bath steam and in the warmth of his attention. John would listen, make sympathetic noises, and be happy you were home.

You never argued in those years of marriage, you tell me. Perhaps with your airline jobs you were never home together enough…But really, it sounds beautiful, the way you tell it. The little house on Hazel Street, a trellis on the south wall hanging heavy with your roses. A yard just big enough for flying John's model planes. And so many plans: four children, a little sailboat, a cottage on a lake.

"Only once he yelled at me," you've told me. On the choppy waters of Lake Opeongo in Algonquin Park. "Paddle, dammit!" he shouted above the storm that was threatening to swamp the canoe. Blown ashore in the rain and darkness at an abandoned, bear-frequented portage, he put you inside the tent and set it up around you. And then, after a shivering night, he had the audacity to give away the coffee rations to another pair of lost campers who happened past the tent.

"But," you say, "that was his style. Fed strays, always picked up hitch-hikers—I loved him for it."

He loved you too, I know it. I see it in his eyes as they smile at you in the photos, or into the camera you must have been holding. But he told Auntie Heather…I'm hesitant to share this with you. He told his sister that marriage was not how he'd imagined it to be.

We can never know what he meant, of course. Perhaps he'd realized just how many of his passions you weren't able to share. You couldn't swim, ski, sail, camp or play bridge, try as you did to learn these things.

But I'm sure all that didn't matter. You were passionately in love. I see it in every photograph of the two of you—in your eyes, in the way your bodies come together in the frame, the comfortable intimacy marked by an arm wrapped snugly around relaxed shoulders, a hand resting lightly on a knee.

He even got on well with Oma. Cooked for her, if only bacon and eggs.

So what if things weren't perfect the way you remember them? Why would I want to interrogate your best memories? No. It's not necessary. It wouldn't be fair. And besides, this way I can have had a perfect father.

AT THE KNOCK ON THE DOOR downstairs, I jump off the *Federbett*. "That's probably my boyfriend."

"Oh?" says Oma, "I didn't know he was coming." I sit back down beside her.

"Oh, Oma, yes you did. And later he's taking me away for the weekend, I know I've told you." I hear my mother welcoming him inside, and I fidget, knowing Oma is not yet finished with me.

"So when you stay at night, where do you sleep? Does he have a place for you?"

"Oh, Oma, where do you think we sleep when we go camping?" I try to keep my voice level.

She looks at me. Her face is unreadable.

"*Ha,* together. *Wie zwei verheiratete.*" She sighs.

I sigh too, and go to the door. What to say? My hand on the door-knob, I turn. "No, Oma, not like 'married people,' like people in love." It is the best I can do.

She laughs sharply. "Love is nice when you are still young. When you get to be my age you see how short love is. How love really is."

I hear my boyfriend's laugh, and run down the stairs.

"THE OLD ONES THEY COLLECTED in the last days," Oma said. Onkel Frank was in town for the afternoon. We were chatting over coffee and *Gugelhupf*—marble poundcake. He had brought his mother flowers—pink and yellow and red carnations. I've always thought them ugly. Alexander used to call them funeral flowers.

"Everyone said, *Die alten Affen sind Hitler seine neuen Waffen*—the old apes are Hitler's new weapons. So your Opa had to enlist. It was '44."

"I didn't know he fought, Oma," I said, setting the vase on the table.

"Oh, he never made it to the front."

"The army came and said you gotta go, so he went," said Frank. "They spent a week in St. Gottard, and the other men all said they were volunteers. My dad said to himself, 'I'm not a volunteer. I had to come.' Then they put them into the cattle cars and headed into Hungary for training. What happened was that the planes came and started bombing the train, so they all had to jump out into the fields.

My dad said to himself, 'Now wait a minute, I'm not a volunteer,' and when the all-clear sounded he didn't get back on that train."

"This was outside of Sombathey," Oma said, her spoon loud against the ceramic mug. "And from there they fled, he and his neighbour. They went home by foot. It took three or four days of walking. But during the day they hid themselves in cornfields, and walked when it was dark. He came home. Our neighbour, he hid himself, no one knew he was back, but Franz, he said '*Awasch*,' and worked hard like before. He went to St. Gottard to get something, and there the SS saw him. Those disgusting dogs." They exchanged a look. Frank blew steam across his mug.

"So Dad was home for three, four weeks. Then one night, I think it was four, five in the morning, I heard the door crash open, and men with searchlights ran into the house. The SS had it circled."

"I didn't know what was happening," Oma said, "and suddenly there was a bright light in my eyes, and then I saw they had a gun to his head."

"To Dad's head." Frank interjected.

"You saw?" Oma was startled.

"Oh, *ja*, I saw. I hid behind the door."

Oma gazed at her son, pensive. "'This man is a deserter,' the SS officer said in his fancy German. There were three of them in the room. 'Here,' I said, 'here I am too. Go ahead, shoot me, too.' And we stared at each other across the bed." Oma's voice was low, even.

"Oh, *ja*, your Oma, she had guts, I tell you," Frank said. "They were gonna shoot him right there, I know it, and her too. That's what they did to people who wouldn't work for them."

"But then, *der grausliger Hund*, he took the gun and reached across to me. With the gun he pulled my nightdress open. Just at the top. Not to look, *nit*, just to show he could. The metal was cold on my skin. I didn't move."

"And then Dad said, 'Leave her alone.' And then I was sure he was a dead man. But there was a noise from outside, and they took him away."

"*Ja*," Oma said, "and so they took him away. And the next day I went up to the *Kasern*, to the jail where they had locked him up. I went on

82

my bicycle to him, and took him food, as much as I could carry, and clothes. And he and the others were taken away by train in the night on October twenty-fourth, 1944. They didn't know where they would end up. And he didn't come back, and I could find out nothing."

"Wait a minute," I paused, my hand on the coffee pot, "that's my mom's birthday…"

"Yup, it is," Frank said and smiled.

"*Ja,* so and then I bicycled home," Oma continued, "and Erika was born."

"How far would you say the *Kasern* was, twenty kilometres?" Frank asked, pretending to ignore my stunned expression.

"*Ja, sauwos,* something like that. I barely made it off my bicycle, didn't have time to find the midwife. I was hardly on the bed and she was here already."

I am eight years old. It is windy on the green mountain, but the air is still warmer than inside the chapel, with its massive stone walls and low door-ways, where you, Erika, were just married to Alexander. Alexander Kummer. The translation of "Kummer" is "trouble." Didn't that worry you?

From up on the Auerberg the red-roofed Bavarian villages dotting the valley look like they have been lifted from my Sleeping Beauty picture book. And I wonder how much of this memory is the stuff of fairy tales, it seems so perfect. The bells of St. Georg's begin to ring, and the bells from the valley answer in celebration.

The local people have blocked the road down the mountain, and have invited the wedding guests to form a circle. Grey cows with loud bells and long eyelashes watch through fence rails as the people dance local dances in your honour — Schuhplattler, Ländler. I twirl with them, making up the steps, a little girl for once not shy, ribbons bouncing around my face — there is a photo. Then the circle clears and the Brautpaar is called forward. A violin and an accordion play a simple waltz. You glide with him around the circle in your smooth, off-white dress. Your favourite daisies are in your bouquet this time, not in your hair. Your eyes are locked, and you are both smiling, softly. I watch and wonder if he'll want me to call him "Daddy."

Oma comes and takes my hand, and together we sway to the music. I look up and see that her cheek is wet, but I cannot tell if she is happy or sad.

I GUIDE MY BOYFRIEND'S FINGERS on the keys. Sunny major triads, then stormy minor tones vibrate through the old piano and bounce off the living-room walls. We lean into each other and laugh at the music we are making. His free hand rests lightly on my back. I stretch my leg across his to reach the pedals. Playing.

Suddenly, his hand drops and he shifts away. I look up from the keys into Oma's face. She has soundlessly materialized from the kitchen and stands watching us, her lips pulled into a weary smile.

Oma has always had this habit of sneaking up on people. It drives me crazy. When I say I'm going to study, or read, or take a nap, I know she will come to "check on me." She still does this whenever I am home. Sometimes I'll look up from my desk and see her eyes in the crack between the door and the hinge. When I catch her watching me, she says with a smile, *"E hamma denkt, E muss schaun gehn, woas inser Mädl macht."* I had to see what our girl was doing.

There is no concept of privacy in our house.

When I was little I used to read in bed with a flashlight, the whole bit, with one ear always waiting for the soft brush of the hallway door being opened. I had the breathing of sleep down pat. I faked it so well that my own body was often fooled. I'd wake up in the morning with the flashlight and the book pressing into my side.

"Dinner is almost ready," Oma says.

"I know," I reply irritably. The spicy smell of *Gulasch* bubbling on the stove surrounds us. "But Oma, we are still leaving right after dinner." Food is her first strategy for keeping me home. After dinner she will decide that it is far too late for us to be driving away — you never know what might happen in the dark.

"Ask him if he will eat *Gulasch,*" Oma says in German, looking at my boyfriend.

"Ask him yourself, Oma!" She is so shy with her English around him. And I want so much for these two people I love to communicate.

"Ha," she says, chuckling, *"Mochts a Gulasch essen?"*

I sigh loudly and let my head drop onto his shoulder.

"Um, yes, of course I'd love to eat," he guesses bravely. "I'm very hungry."

"Gut!" She gives him a bright smile and turns to go.

I kiss him impulsively, and suddenly Oma is back.

"Another thing I wanted to tell you. It's all nice and good to be like this at the beginning, so close and in love. But you never know, in a minute it will be gone, that love. Just like that, it will vanish." She presses her hands together, lets them spring apart. "*Pfuff,* like that. And then? What will you have then?" She looks at us gravely. "The most important thing is that *ihr könnt einander gut leiden. Gut leiden.* You have to compromise and accept each other and all your problems, because love, that leaves. Early, soon, it leaves." Her tone is not malicious, not sad. Just matter-of-fact. Somehow this makes her words harder to take.

"Oh, Oma. It doesn't have to be that way," I say. "If you know someone really well…"

"You can never know," she interjects with finality. "Just wait. You'll see."

THE PINK, YELLOW AND RED CARNATIONS Frank had brought were already drooping. I took them to the sink and made a fresh cut across their stems.

"Finally in the spring, after so many months, a letter arrived," said Oma.

Onkel Frank had finished his coffee and left for home. The sun was low in the trees and its light was soft on our faces, on the kitchen walls. Oma and I began to wash the coffee dishes. Her hands in the water were a mess of blue and purple marks, like bruised fruit. 'Fragile,' the doctor calls her waxy, translucent skin. Fragile is not a word for my Oma.

"A letter from my Opa?"

"*Ja,*" Oma said. "He wrote that he was in Austria, in Gmunden, in a prisoner of war camp where the English were. I decided to try and see him, to go up there across the two borders with Resi—my sister, *nit*. We had to cross the Russian border, we had to smuggle ourselves across, and over the English border too. It was so tricky, *nit,* because no one could know where you were going, who you were. We argued about our identity passes, but we did take them. If they are going to shoot us, they'll shoot us, I said, pass or no pass."

I watched the steam rise from the drying rack and waited until the plates were cool enough for me to touch. I could see Oma and her younger sister conspiring over dishwater, their heads bent close in the steam.

"And so early in the morning when there were still stars, we went to Jenischdorf on foot. We took only a little money, *nit,* and our *Rucksäck* with cheese and bread *drin.* And there at the train station we asked how to get to Gmunden. The engineer, he was good. He wrote everything down for us, but he told us we could not betray him. He knew, he said, when a train was coming up from Ungarn, and in St. Gotthard was the first border into Austria. He knew the crew, he said, and he would ask them to take us. They put us up front in the locomotive and covered us with the black coal sacks. *Pfui* — so noisy and smelly it was in there." Oma wrinkled her nose and pursed her lips.

"And then the train slowed and we were at the checkpoint. I felt Resi trembling beside me and I tried to breathe in only a little air. Here they come, the coal man warned us quietly. The Russian soldiers came on board, and the coal man, he tried to joke with them. I didn't hear a reply. But I could see their black boots. And then a boot came down on Resi's *Rucksack* where it lay under the sacks, and I stopped breathing." She paused and squinted into the sun. Added more hot water to the suds.

"But they were quick with their inspection. And then we were off again. The crew took us as far as they could, and then they left us in a field at the edge of a wood. I remember the coal man waving and blowing kisses at us as the train pulled away. That's when we looked at each other and realized that we were all black. Our clothes, our hair, our faces. I remember how wild Resi looked." Oma shook her head slowly, laughing. "We sat there in the field and she pulled out the bread stomped on by the Russian. *Ja,* so wild she looked, grinning at me with her bright eyes and teeth and messed up hair. I guess I looked the same."

I met Resi when we were in Budapest in 1993. It was so strange. Like meeting another Oma, but smaller, frailer. And to see them together after so many years was…well, it made me wish I had a sister.

"And so then there was another border to cross. At a farmhouse we asked how and where."

"You just walked up and asked?"

"Oh no," Oma laughed. "Of course not. We hid in the grass until we saw that there was just a woman there. Then we risked it. She helped us. She told us where the patrols walk and where and when we had to go. There was a high mountain and a forest, and snow still. We went up part of the mountain and somehow got over the border. I only remember hearing gunshots somewhere behind us, and falling on a root, and then running and running and hoping the snow would not be as loud as it sounded to me. We were so lucky. And at the second station past the border, we caught a train, and so we got to Gmunden."

AFTER OMA'S LOVE LECTURE, she melts back into the kitchen, and I attack the keyboard. I play a strong yat-da yat-da Hungarian melody, dark and passionate. The picture frames on top of the piano rattle with each chord. I am angry at no one in particular.

My boyfriend stops my hands. Gently.

"So?" he says. I don't take my hands from the keys.

"So what did she say?" he asks, not removing his hands from mine. Oma had addressed us both, but in German. He didn't understand a word, naturally. Sometimes I forget to let him in.

"You know," I stall, pointing to the photographs, "sometimes I choose one of them and send him my music. I pretend they can hear it." My father is there in a frame, smiling and handsome in his pilot's uniform. Alexander with his mischievous eyes is there, too.

My boyfriend is waiting in silence.

Deciding how to translate Oma's lecture seems tremendously important. Her words press on my brain. I take a deep breath.

"She says," I tell him, "that falling out of love is inevitable."

He wrinkles his forehead. "Why does she think that? I don't understand that. Not at all."

"She says," I continue, "that we had best learn to tolerate each other." He is shaking his head, grinning. Suddenly it is funny. He hugs me and we laugh and the piano bench creaks. My head falls back and I look up into my father's eyes.

"Did you know my father was your age when he died?" I say, pulling away. "Twenty-eight years old. It's such a jinx. Women in my family have no luck with men."

"You don't think you're lucky?" he quips. "Just to have me for a little while?"

"Aren't you scared?" I have to ask.

"No. Not at all."

"IT WAS RAINING AND SNOWING when we got to Gmunden," Oma said. "And everything was wet and grey. The sky, the buildings, the people. Everything grey. We didn't know where the camp was and we were soaking wet, so we went into a *Wirtshaus.* 'Where do you have your cards?' the woman said when I asked about food. You could get nothing to eat there without these *Lebensmittel* cards. When she saw I didn't know about them she looked around and quickly gave us soup. 'Don't worry about the cards,' she whispered, and tilted her head toward the tables. There were soldiers eating there, I think they were *Engländer.* And so we had to be careful and pretend we were locals. The good thing about the rain is that it washed most of the coal dust away. And grey clothes were normal.

"That good woman told us where the camp was. When we went there they made us register, but they wouldn't let us in on that day. It was dark by then, and we were so exhausted and cold, and we didn't know where to sleep. So we wandered around the city. I worried about a curfew. Then a Hungarian officer—they were stationed there, *woarst*—came and Resi spoke good Hungarian, and he took us in."

"Just like that?" I asked. The Hungarians changed sides in the war; by 1945, if you spoke German, they were the "enemy."

"*Ha,* Resi was a beautiful girl, *nit.* That helped. We were soaking wet, our shoes, our stockings. He had a servant, a man who fired up the stove and made us tea, and dried our stockings. I didn't like having bare legs like that, but what could we do, *nit?* This officer had a room with two beds, pushed together. All three of us slept there that night. We didn't exactly sleep, it was enough to lie there out of the cold. I was in the middle, and his breath so close made me feel sick, but I didn't want to move. Resi, she was a beautiful girl, *nit,* and he kept trying to reach over me to get at her, and I kept batting his arm away. It was the longest night."

The last year I lived at home I remember being with Oma when the letter arrived from Budapest. She read it quickly, then carefully folded it into a tiny square and tucked it into her apron. She went up to her room and closed the door. Somehow I knew then that Resi had died.

"In the morning we went to the camp. There I told them who I wanted to see. And then he came." Oma pulled the sink plug. Paused while the water drained away.

"He came, and I didn't recognize him. He was completely bloated. They weren't being given anything to eat. They ate the grass, he said, every blade of grass was plucked from the earth at that prison camp."

I stared at her in silence. She was far away. There was nothing to say. She closed her eyes and sighed as if she were forcing every molecule of air from her lungs.

"*Ja. Und* so, then we went home again," she said.

"You went through all that just to see him?"

"*Ha ja,* of course."

"But if it was so dangerous…"

"Oh, *ja,* it was dangerous," she said quickly. "We were lucky to get through."

I thought of my mother, five months old. And Frank and Rudi, too. "Then why risk it, Oma?"

"*Ha,* he was my *Mann,* my husband. I loved him and I was worried."

There was silence. Oma gazed intently at the last of the bubbles in the sink. Then she folded her dishcloth and disappeared upstairs.

"ALL RIGHT YOU TWO, enough smooching," my mother says, swooping into the living room. "Laura, can I talk to you for a minute?" She gives my boyfriend her best airline smile. I notice she is wearing fresh lipstick.

"Coming," I say, and slide off the piano bench.

"That's better," she breathes when we are alone upstairs. "I can't talk to you if you two are always intertwined."

"We are not!" I shoot back before I catch the mirth in her expression. "Jealousy," I add, "will get you nowhere."

She laughs, and shows me the boxes of clothes she "needs" me to look through, right then before I go. "I am," she announces, "trying to unclutter my life."

"But these aren't my clothes..." I mutter plaintively. It is getting late. I could swear they are working as a team to keep me at home.

"No, they're Alexander's. See if you want anything."

I pull out a faded plaid shirt and hug it to my chest.

"Mom, were you always sure you were in love?"

She looks at me. "Well, yes. Of course. When I was, I was sure."

"Oma just said that it can't ever last..."

"Oma said?" She collapses dramatically into a chair. "Don't get me started. I don't know if she has ever been in love. What does she know about it? Just what it says in those cheap German romances she reads all the time, they're horrible. They put all sorts of crazy ideas in her head."

"But you buy them for her," I say.

She looks at me strangely. Her eyes narrow. "You aren't thinking of getting married or something, are you? You would tell me first, wouldn't you?"

I groan. "I just want to have your opinion, that's all."

She examines her fingernails intently. "Love is amazing, but..."

"But?"

"But maybe Oma has a point," she says carefully.

"What do you mean?"

"Look, all I'm saying is that people change. They do."

You thought you knew him so well, Mom. Guess you underestimated the stress of switching countries, continents, languages. Not that Alexander wasn't up for an adventure. He lived for it, almost, and I loved to tag along.

Sunday afternoons when you were flying he'd say, "Hey, miss, let's go on an adventure." We would grab some granola bars and head north. How many roadside forests did we get "lost" in? Oma would scold us at length when we arrived home after dark, gleefully dirty and covered in burrs. "I already saw you dead in a ditch, or drowned, or in the hospital..." on and on. Alexander would apologize, sort of, and wink at me. He had this way of winking that left his face totally still, so you could only catch it if it was meant for you.

I don't know how things were between you two at the beginning. Good, I'm sure. Kids pick up on bad vibes quickly. I don't remember when we stopped going on our adventures, but I bet it coincided with my problems sleeping through the night.

I remember waking up, disoriented in the dark, to harsh whispers in German. During the day we spoke only English, to help him learn. But in the dark, always German. Ugly bursts of words from your bedroom. I'd catch my name and be so alarmed that your arguing should be about me. Always, it seemed.

"You shouldn't let her do that..."

"And what do you know about raising my daughter?"

"Obviously more than you do. Just listen to her at the table, she's so spoiled she never knows when to shut up."

"Oh, so it's all my fault, is it? How do I know what goes on when I'm at work? Oma's had her hand in from the start..."

"She's your daughter, you just said it yourself."

Silence.

"Well if you would just show a little initiative and find a job, you'd be a better influence."

"Oh, so now I'm the problem. Maybe I should have just stayed in Germany, eh?"

"Maybe. We were fine without you, just fine..."

And the insults and accusations would get louder, go on and on. In the next room, ringed by stuffed animals, I lay as though paralysed, listening. I couldn't not listen. Eventually I would break free to get up and shut the door. Slam it sometimes, wanting you to know I was awake, that I'd heard. Some mornings I would see him emerge from the spare bedroom.

Nothing was ever, ever mentioned about these nights. But when I saw you mark the calendar with a red X in the following September I knew, without you ever telling me, why it was there.

"SO OMA, YOU NEVER WANTED to get married again?" I asked her once.

"No."

"Never ever?"

"No. I could have married a couple of times. But I said, I won't marry until my children are grown. Until they can earn their own bread, I said, and until they no longer are dependent on me. I don't want a stepfather for my children."

"Why not?"

"*Ha,* because I saw that those children had nothing good. The ones with stepmothers or fathers. Alexander was good. He was really good to you, *nit,* as far as it went, but if you had had another, who didn't want you…" She shrugged.

"One man wanted to marry me, he had four children. I said, 'Listen. You have four and I have three, that makes seven.' '*Ja,*' he said, 'Mine are all grown, they will marry and leave and I'll be alone.' I said, ' I don't care. I don't want to marry.' And then there was another one, he wanted to have me too, and I said, 'No, I won't marry until my children are grown and can earn their own bread.'

"So I stayed alone. I don't regret it yet, that I was alone. I had lots of work, *nit.* Like your mother, too, *Kummer und Sorgen,* troubles and worries you have enough of, when you are married. And when you are alone. But when you are alone, no one can say anything to you. No one can tell you how to live your life."

WHEN I COME DOWNSTAIRS with my pack, I see they have my boyfriend cornered in the kitchen. I reach between them and grab his hand.

"Come, let's go." I brace myself for what will inevitably come next.

"Do you have enough warm clothes *dabei?*" asks Oma.

"Do me a favour and at least brush your hair before you go," says my mother.

"Are you wearing an undershirt at least? It's cold."

"I bet you're forgetting your toothbrush, do you have your toothbrush? And try, won't you, to stop biting your nails…"

"Call when you get there!"

We wade through their words to the door. I turn to my boyfriend. "Remind me again how old I am…"

In his truck I slump in the seat. He is laughing softly. "Do *me* a favour and brush your hair—"

"Please, let's just go."

They are standing at the windows, one on either side of the door.

"I wish it didn't always feel as though I were stealing you away from them," he says.

I say nothing. He knows I cannot change this.

"So what were they telling you just now?" I ask as I shift the bags of food Oma has given him to my feet. The *Gulasch* is still warm.

"Your Oma says that I shouldn't let you tell me what to do. Your mother says that I should stand up for what I want."

"Jeeez!" I slump further.

He looks at me with his hand on the key and grins. "So let's get married."

My laughter is drowned out by the truck's rattling engine.

Horse stories

"*M*AM, DO YOU WANNA COME grocery shopping?" Frank asks, twirling the keys to the truck.

"Let's all go," I suggest.

Frances takes the keys from Frank's hand. "I'll drive," she says.

I look at her with wide eyes. "You've learned?"

"Got the license her first try," Frank says. "At fifty-eight, think of that."

"*Ja,*" Frances says, "I decided that since we live up here now, so far away from everything, I better learn." To me she whispers, "I've never felt so free in all my life."

On the way into town we zip through towering rock cuts, the ancient granite exposed like giant wounds in the landscape. Oma grips the door. "*Fohr na nit so schnell!*" she scolds. Frances decelerates slightly.

The road slices through endless forest, curves around the glacial lakes that stud the landscape like pools of liquid sapphire. Someday I will live up here.

Frank is chuckling to himself. "I can still hear Rudi complaining about the distances," he says. "Around the corner can be an hour away for us. But he loves it over here. Didn't want to leave last time. I think he wishes he'd left Germany like the rest of us."

At the general store in Wilberforce we pull up beside a pickup with a horse trailer attached. Its occupants stamp with impatience or hunger, and the trailer shakes.

"My boyfriend wants me to take him horseback riding," I announce.

"So you've found one who understands you, that's good," Frances says.

"*Ja,* where is this man of yours?" Frank asks. "I thought you were gonna bring him."

"He had to work," I lie.

"On the weekend?"

"Yeah. But he really wants to meet you," I assure him. In time, I think. Let him get used to my mother and Oma first.

The general store is surprisingly well stocked, with everything from aspirin to zucchini neatly displayed. So ordered, clean, I think, so very…

"Hallo, Frank," says the clerk, "*wie geht's?*"

…German. I laugh out loud.

While Frank wanders off toward the hardware section, I follow Frances and Oma to the food. Frances chooses sausage, sauerkraut, Pop-tarts. When she reaches for a carton of skim milk, Oma frowns.

"How can you drink that stuff?" she says. "It's thin as water. It looks blue."

"Oh, Oma," I say, "it's good for you."

"I don't trust it," she says, still frowning.

While Frank and Frances chat with the man who serves as both store clerk and postmaster, Oma and I wait on a bench outside. The horse trailer is just leaving.

"We had horses *da Hoam.* Such good horses," she says.

I nod. "Rigo and Linche, right?"

"*Ja,* and others, too.

"In the beginning of the war, before the Russians came, the Hungarians, they were still fighting with the Germans. There were German soldiers *bei uns,* and Hungarians. Later, they fought against each other. But before the Russians came, the war wasn't where we were, except for the soldiers, the officers who strutted around like little gods. We tried to live like before, as much as we could, planting everything *und des oalles.*

"Then one morning I walked into the stable to feed the animals, and there was a Hungarian officer in there with the horses. He looked at me, then he ignored me and started bridling them. A short, burly man he was. With big fleshy hands he fumbled with the buckles. I said, 'What are you doing?' He stopped and looked at me like I was stupid. 'I'm taking these horses,' he said.

"Now, Rigo, he was a good horse, strong and obedient, but he was nervous, *nit,* especially with strange men, and he started snorting and trying to get away. The other horse, she started acting up, too. Come and help me, the officer shouted at me, but I said no. 'No, we need them and I won't give them to you,' I said, 'no.' And I folded my arms and stood there watching the sweat on his face as he tried to get those horses. It was one big stall they were in, *nit,* and they had room to run from him, around and around. Finally he gave up. Kicked Rigo in the belly, and left the stable. I followed him out.

"In the yard, he turned and came at me. 'When the war is over,' he hissed through his teeth, 'I will come and find you,' he said, 'and I'll shoot you. The first bullet belongs to you.' So I said right in his face, 'OK, you can shoot me right away'."

"Oma!"

"Just then we heard Rigo kicking at the stall door. He was hungry, *nit.* The soldier turned and left. Some Germans on the street, they had heard him arguing with me. The one German, also an officer, asked me what he had wanted. 'He wanted the horses,' I said. 'What did he say to you?' he asked. And so I told him that he said he'd shoot me, *nit,* and he got really mad. 'Which one was it?' he asked, and pulled out his gun, and started loading it right there. 'I don't know,' I said quickly, 'they all look the same.'

"Later my mother came with my sisters Milli and Resi, and another Hungarian officer, a good one, and they took the horses. Because they were taking our mam and Milli and Resi with them. The Russians were coming, and the Hungarian soldiers had to move on, they couldn't stop the war. They hitched our horses to the wagon, and they fled as far as Salzburg."

The image of that threatening Hungarian officer is stuck in my mind. "Oma, he could have killed you!" I say. "Why did you keep saying dangerous things?"

"*Ha,*" Oma shrugs. "It was like this: you said something, you got killed. You said nothing, you got killed. Survival in war is only luck. Survival at all is only ever luck."

We sit in silence and watch two crows in the parking lot arguing over the remains of a sandwich.

"When the war was over," Oma begins again, "Milli and Resi and Mam came home from Salzburg in '46. They came back with Hungarian soldiers who had horses. Big strong military horses, dark brown that shone red in the sun. And the Hungarian soldiers gave the horses to our mam, because they said they couldn't use them. I still had enough *Heu und Stroh,* and empty stalls, and so I had those two horses. Milli and Resi often drove them to St. Gotthard to go shopping. And when we went once, some officers saw them and recognised them as Hungarian military horses. They said they'd come and pick them up. 'OK,' I said."

Oma leans toward me in the empty parking lot, and says in a half-whisper, "Milli's friends, though, they were smugglers. And so we arranged that they would come in the night, and would take the horses in exchange for lard. I don't remember any more how much. And flour they gave us, so we had something to eat. I knew when they were coming, I knew the whole plan, but your mother and Rudi and Frank, they didn't know. And my mother-in-law, she was there too, *nit,* but everything was in secret. So the next morning I got up and went to our neighbour. '*Du,*' I said—he was a half communist, *nit*—I said, '*du,* they stole our horses in the night.' 'No,' he said. 'Yes,' I said. 'I heard nothing, and they are gone.'

"Then I saw him leave for town, and soon after, the military came, and wrote everything down, and said I must know something, but I said I know nothing. Then they went and asked Milli and Resi, and then they herded us up to Fidisch, and locked us up for the whole day in the jail. Oh, how it stunk in there! And Rudi and your mother and Frank, they were home alone all day. Then they interrogated us again, saying we must know, we must know where the horses went. But we said we don't know and we don't know. Just think, such a fuss they were making over those horses. In 1946.

"At night they let us go home, because Milli said I had three small children alone at home, with nothing to eat, why don't they let us go home? So they let us. We never said where those horses went.

"Then the smugglers brought us a cow, so I would have milk for the children. And that cow was pregnant, and had a small calf, and no one knew. Everything was so secret. Then the smugglers butchered the calf in the stable, at three or four weeks. Because they weren't allowed to have it, and I wasn't either. They took the cow away, and gave me the meat from the calf. I cooked it, and roasted it, so we had something to eat. They divided and prepared the meat right there in the stable. We took out the straw and washed away the blood so no one could tell.

"What would the neighbour have done?" I ask.

"He would have told on me again, and I might have been locked up again. I don't know what they would have done."

"Nice neighbour."

"I know." She laughs. "But that's how they were. He's already dead, hah hah. They are all already dead." Her otherwise plain tone is mildly triumphant. She straightens and sighs.

"What we all did to get food in those times, you wouldn't believe. And so life went on, until we were deported."

On the way back to the cottage, I ask Frank about the local post-master.

"Heinrich? *Ja,* he's German. From Czechoslovakia before the war." Frank chuckles. "We're everywhere up here in lake country. There's even a club. If you find a house deep in the woods, chances are good that they're Austrian."

THREE

Parting

Mothers-in-Law

"*D*A HOAM," OMA SAYS, "we had two bread-baking days. And on those days, I would get up and *die Schwiegermutter,* my husband's mother, *nit,* she would be waiting for me in the kitchen already. We would light the fire and the lamps, because it was still dark, especially in the winter. It was cold, but we were lucky, we had a wood floor. Not like the house I grew up in, the one you saw, it had packed dirt. That was cold, even with the rugs.

"My mother-in-law slept in the kitchen, *nit,* where she wanted to. So she could keep her eyes on everything. Oh, she hated me. She had a face like you make from sour milk, that woman. But big she was, and fat! She grew fat from scolding. And when you are always mad at everyone, it gives you gas. Her daughter lived with us, too, Cecilia, with Eddie her husband. Everyone called her Celi. She hated me, too.

"But it was my responsibility to make the bread. So I would get up and we would make the dough together, and then I would knead it. For eight loaves I kneaded, eight loaves as big as our *Backofen* could take. We had farm hands to feed as well as the family, *nit.* In the kitchen was a thick wood table. The dough covered the whole top, and I kneaded my way around that table, and my mother-in-law, she watched me. I kneaded until my arms shook and the dough felt tough as cement. But I couldn't stop until she was happy with it. She would poke it, and shake her head, no. Then when I was finished, I would take my things and walk to work. It took an hour to reach the factory when there was no snow. My shift began at seven. And so it went, *nit.*"

The only time we ever ate in the dining room was when my Grandma and Grandpa Taylor came for dinner. You would get out the china plates, dust them off and slip them into the plate warmer. I would fold napkins and dip the silverware into the jar of cleaner. And Oma would spend hours in the kitchen making Schnitzel or Sauerbraten. You would be in the kitchen, too, cracking open rarely used cookbooks to make devilled eggs, a fine cream sauce for the vegetables, a fancy dessert, like pears Hélène or crème caramel.

And then they would come, and Fletch would pour Gerry a scotch and soda in a crystal glass with ice. Geraldine Elise and Fletcher Vaughn Taylor. I would bring out the tray of appetizers, tiny quiches or rows of crackers and cheese. It was my role to entertain until the meal was ready, so I would sit and field the inevitable questions about school and my future career plans. Go for the money, Grandpa would say with a wink. A tall, gentle man with shaggy eyebrows, and a deep chuckle. Grandma, her figure still trim and shapely after three children, would scold her husband for eating too many appetizers, and would smother me with praise. As you know, she'd say, patting my hand, we are so very proud of you, Laura Elise. Their oldest grandchild. Her favourite, as everyone knew.

You sparkled on those evenings. I tried to imitate the ease, the casual elegance of your demeanour: the way you held your wine glass, the way you could serve vegetables between two serving spoons held in one hand, the way you could answer Grandma's prying questions about your love life with a smile and diplomatic evasion. The perfect hostess.

I learned, slowly, to play my part, to slip into this world of salad and dessert forks and pretend to be comfortable in it.

Oma stayed in the kitchen as much as she could without seeming rude. I'm sure she felt that there was no room at that table for her. She would smile and greet them, but always held herself apart. Ha, she'd say, what do I have to say to those people?

When the meal was over, Grandma would praise the food effusively, and praise you for being such a wonderful hostess, such a wonderful person. One of my favourite people, she'd say.

"OMA, WHY DID your mother-in-law hate you?"

"*Die Schwiegermutter?* Ha, she came from rich farmers. She married a rich farmer. She didn't want my husband to marry me. Because I was poor.

"*Ja*, she wanted rich to marry rich, so the rich would get richer. I said to her once, I said, you should think about where poor people come from. The poor people come from the rich ones. Because the rich ones give everything to just one son, and the others have nothing, the others are all poor. The poor come from the rich.

"And that's why I had to work at the factory. Because I had nothing, I brought nothing into the marriage, so I had to work. *Die Schwiegermutter*, she owned part of my husband's farm. She wasn't his mother, though. His father married twice before he died, so she was my husband's stepmother. We were saving money up to buy her out. So much work," she says, closing her fists. "And we lost it all in the end, anyways, in the war."

I wonder what went through Oma's head when she learned that her daughter was going to marry the son of a Canadian bomber pilot. During Grandpa Taylor's tour of duty, his plane was shot down, he was smuggled by the French Underground into Switzerland, and he completed daring reconnaissance missions into German territory. It makes for an exciting story, doesn't it? He won't speak of it often. But he is quite sure, he says, that none of his bombing runs went as far as the Hungarian border.

A veteran at twenty-four and back home in Saskatchewan, he joined Trans Canada Airlines, and married his sweetheart. Geraldine Elise Wilson was quite the girl. "The redheaded wonder of Saskatchewan," they called her. I have a newspaper photo of her at nineteen, in shorts and a T-shirt, posing with her feet in starting blocks on the track at the University of Saskatchewan. Thick curls frame strong, attractive features. Balanced by fingertips on the gravel track, her toned body is coiled in mock readiness. Together with her mother, she was doubles Tennis champion of Saskatchewan in 1939. If they hadn't cancelled the Olympics in 1940, she would have represented Canada in running and shot put.

Do you remember the summer you signed me up for a week of tennis lessons? 'She's a natural,' the instructor gushed after the first day. But I felt out of place. The same way I feel when Grandma and Grandpa take us out to the golf club for dinner. I look at the waiters, all my age, with their plastic smiles and the deferential, fawning attitude expected of them in that place, and I lose my appetite. You tell me not to be silly, to enjoy the unfamiliar decadence, at least enjoy the food. But I can't. I don't know why. Oma always declines Grandpa's invitations.

"ONCE," SAYS OMA, "I had not been married very long, when *die Schwiegermutter* went to visit in another town overnight, and took Celi with her. She did this on purpose, nit, to see if I could control her kitchen without her. Eddie stayed, though, and he helped me. He was a good one, Eddie was. I don't know why he married Celi.

"We baked the bread together. And when she came back, she didn't say *hallo* to me, not to no one, before she went looking for the bread. I was proud of that bread. It rose so beautifully. She found it on the racks, and she put her hands on those cooling loaves, and then, you know what she did then? She pounded on them with all her strength, so mad she was.

"Eddie watched all this, and he was laughing. 'Go away, mother,' he said. 'You don't need to come home, Laura can do it just as good as you.' Oh, was she mad. So mad. You know what we say in German? *'Alle Tag' Versollen, nur der Teufel soll die Schwiegermutter holen'*. I would eat beans every day, if the devil would take my mother-in-law away. That woman could really make my life hell.

"So, Laura," Oma continues, "when you marry it's best you don't go and live with the parents."

"People don't do that here. I'll live where I want."

Oma smiles at me sagely. *"Ha,* you never know," she says. *"Bei uns* it wasn't like that. If you were poor, you had no choice. You were happy if someone would have you. You had to tolerate or suffer wherever you ended up. Where else would you have gone?"

I find it curious that among my favourite meals are two that you make. The only two that you make: stroganoff and lasagne. Both are tasty, but they require planning, as the recipes call for ingredients not found in Oma's kitchen. It's amusing, don't you think, how quickly Oma disappears when you get out the recipe cards. I can see you setting the cards, tomato sauce-splattered and yellowing, on the counter by the stove. The original, flowing script on the cards belongs to Grandma Taylor, right? I find it interesting that, after all these years, you still need the directions. The writing has been marked up with your changes — less water, more tomatoes. But what if you were to change the ingredients one of these days. Add some spinach, perhaps, or paprika...

"WHEN I WAS AT THE FACTORY, *die Schwiegermutter* watched the children, *nit*. She was supposed to watch the children. If I hadn't had to go to the factory...*Ja*, if I hadn't had to go, Rudi wouldn't have had the accident.

"Frank was eight, Rudi was six when it happened, I'll never forget. I was at the factory, and it was harvest time. We were threshing, and we had this farm machine in the *Hof* that we used the horses to run — we drove them in a circle, *nit*. A gypsy woman came, selling things, and no one watched what the children were doing. Rudi was running around with the others, and nobody saw what happened until the horses stopped. Then they looked and saw that Rudi was caught in the machine, so the horses couldn't continue. They dragged him out. He was coal black, his foot was broken, and his hands and everything. We didn't have a telephone, so someone had to go to St. Gottard with a bike to get the doctor, who took Rudi to the hospital in his car. He collected me from the factory on the way. I sat with Rudi, but I couldn't touch him. I didn't recognize him. He was coal black and had such a big head."

"Why?"

"Why? Because his feet got stuck so that all his blood was forced to his head. His lower half was bright white and on top he was black with blood, with his eyes bulging out. When the nurse wheeled him away, I said, 'This is not my boy.' I didn't know him at all." Oma is twisting a tissue in her hands as she speaks. Her voice is thick with emotion.

"They laid him on an ice pillow. After two days his colour was normal again. But his foot was broken, and both hands were broken in two places. He stayed in the hospital three, four weeks.

"Then he came home, and his foot wasn't healed underneath yet, and my mother-in-law wouldn't let him wear shoes. Most of the children didn't wear them in the summer, except on Sundays, *nit,* but he was supposed to wear shoes so his foot would heal, and she wouldn't let him wear any."

"Why?" I ask. "You were his mother. Why didn't you explain it to her?"

"She was a…" Oma shakes her head, not finding the words. "And I was in the factory, I didn't know what went on at home. Rudi had to tend cows, *nit,* and it was almost autumn and cool. The grass in the fields was wet, and the foot broke open again. His foot is still open today. *Ja.* He kept going to the hospital and they said he had to always bind it, or he would die. Today still. Last time he was here I asked, and he still binds it."

I've always known of Onkel Rudi's accident. He has to have special shoes made, with one sole much thicker than the other, like a platform shoe, and he walks with the slightly rolling gate of one for whom balance is not a given. When I was little, I imagined the sole of the afflicted foot opening like a cut made in raw meat.

I NEVER HAD A BABY-SITTER. Oma was always there, always watching over my every move. Ready to scold if I went out with wet hair or without a scarf, or if I sat on cold stone (this is bad for women, apparently), or if I ran around after a rain without shoes on.

But she would let me spend most of the summer barefoot. I remember the cool, smooth cement of the garage, the prickles of crabgrass like stubble on a face, digging my toes into the garden earth. I remember sitting on the front steps with Lindsay and Michael, neighbours who would run away from their babysitters to come to our house. We would sit and compare with deep satisfaction the smooth, thick calluses developing on our heels and on the balls of our feet. With these calluses you could go anywhere, we thought. When my mother came home from a flight, I could even run barefoot over the gravel driveway to meet her without wincing. I would bury my face in the smoky airplane smell of her uniform and she would pick me up and hug me and call me uncouth.

Every night I would come in from playing, with skin still warm from the sun. Oma would let me in only as far as the front room. She would sit me down on the green couch and examine my feet, the soles black with ground-in dirt. I would wait while she filled the orange bucket with steaming hot, soapy water. Gingerly I would lower my feet in. The water was so hot it would take my breath away, make my whole body tingle. And then I would slump into an exhausted haze as every muscle melted. Oma would wait until my surrender was complete. Then she would kneel on the moss-green carpet and take each foot in her hands and scrub it with an abrasive brush. I sat in a pleasant daze while she attacked the dirt, and my precious calluses, with vigorous scrubs. It took forever until she reached pink skin. And the next day it would be the same.

How often did we see my grandparents, maybe four times a year? Between bridge club retreats, golf tournaments and winters at the condo in Florida, their social calendar was so full that you scheduled visits months in advance. I was five when Grandpa retired from Air Canada, a 747 captain with four stripes. Impressive. I'm sure they have flown more since then than he did as a pilot. I remember tagging along to water the plants at their apartment when they were away. For years you did this for them.

By the time I was a teenager, I had my role with the grandparents down pat. You and I worked like a tag team, covering for each other, steering the dinner conversations away from difficult subjects, like my father. Grandma would bring up her favourite son at least once. And cry. "Is this too hard to hear, Laura?" you would ask me pointedly. I would nod my head, knowing I was the only one at the table who could handle hearing it. Soon we would have Grandma smiling again, praising the food, praising us.

"That woman is so falsch,*" Oma said almost under her breath as we were cleaning up the kitchen after a dinner. I must have been about fifteen.*

"False? What do you mean, Oma?" I asked.

"Oh, you know. She smiles and smiles but behind your back, watch out." I went to challenge this, but something in her voice held me back.

"Ja," Oma continued, "just ask your mother. Ask your mother how it was for her with your Grandma."

You overheard. "Yes, it was pretty awful at the beginning," you said lightly. "She tried to drive us apart, your father and me, any way she could. But that was a long, long time ago. It's not important." You would not say more.

So I asked my Aunt Heather. She says Grandma took every opportunity to show her son the mistake he was making. Heather remembers evenings of bridge or Scrabble, played at her mother's insistence. On those painful evenings, she doesn't remember hearing you speak.

I can see you, puzzling over these foreign games with a quiet desperation. The letters on your chips refuse to spell out English words.

"There." Grandma smiles as she lays her chips on the board. "D-i-s-s-o-n-a-n-c-e. Dissonance for twenty-two points. Do you know that word, Erika, or must I explain?"

"So Erika, what does your father do?" Grandpa interjects neutrally. Silence. You don't know where to look, how to explain.

John is sitting across the table. "Her father was a landowner in Hungary before the war," he says quickly, and turns the conversation to aircraft. You feel his toes caressing your feet under the table and exhale gratefully. But watching him, so at home in the oversized armchair, one arm draped across the back, a glass of scotch in his hand, you must have wondered. What did he see when he looked across at you, perched on the edge of your chair?

On the way out, when you thank your mother-in-law-to-be for the evening, she pretends not to understand your accent. Turns to her son and whispers, "Johnny, you've always been a smart boy. I don't want to be too blunt, but this is your life. Don't be stupid." I can hear her say this.

I wonder what Oma thought, watching her own Cinderella story repeating itself in you. The story of Aschenputtel: young, attractive but poor girl meets dashing young man with money and good prospects. A bad mix in any culture, from a mother-in-law's perspective.

"WHEN THE RUSSIANS CAME and we had to flee," Oma says, "*die Schwiegermutter* went with Celi to Burgenland somewhere. And after, when we came back, we had nothing, *nit*, only old shrivelled carrots and beets and some potatoes. The neighbours and the Russians had stolen everything. And I had three children to feed, *nit*. It's bad to think about that time.

"For months we heard nothing from *die Schwiegermutter*. She must have known how bad we had it, but she didn't come and didn't come. And then one day she showed up with a bag of flour. She stood on the doorstep, and I thought, she looks old. She let the bag fall to the floor, and a little cloud of flour *ist rausgeflogen*. 'Here, take it,' she said, 'so the children can have bread.' But it was hard to be grateful. Her clothes, the flour, her hair, everything was crawling with lice.

"And then, when we were forced to leave, to go to Germany, she wanted to come with me. 'I can look after the children,' she said, 'so you can go to work.' And I almost took her, *nit. Sie hat mir Leid 'tan.*"

A strange phrase, it means "I felt sorry for her." But literally translated, it becomes "she *made* me feel sorry for her." As if even in defeat, this woman wielded power.

"But, Oma, she was such a witch to you!"

"*Ja*, I know, but I still felt sorry for her. My neighbour, though, she said, 'Don't you dare take that one with you, don't you dare.' I knew she was right. So I didn't. She went to live with Celi for a while, but Celi kicked her out eventually. I don't know where she went after that. I'm sure she's dead now."

So, was it John's death that changed Grandma's mind about you? I imagine so. You and I were all she had left of him, I've heard that often enough. But what about you? In a corner of my brain I have been angry ever since I learned how she treated you, all those years ago. Someday you will have to teach me how you manage to forget. Or forgive. Or whatever it is that you do so well.

Grandma and Grandpa Taylor turn eighty this year. This could well be their last winter in Florida, Grandpa mused when last we saw them. Health insurance soars after eighty, you know. But we know it is because of Grandma that they are home in Mississauga so frequently these days. You noticed the change already two years ago, when Grandpa was so sick and you visited him at the hospital every day. 'I'm worried about Grandma,' you said.

Sitting across from her in the restaurant this last time, I saw that the red has seeped from her hair, leaving a dishevelled grey nest. She looks out at the world with increasingly confused eyes. When I told Oma of how Grandma swore, loudly, at the waitresses in the restaurant, she said, 'You see, the truth in a person always comes out in the end.'

Grandma swears at her husband too, incessantly. You never get used to it, Grandpa says, even when you know she doesn't mean it. That she can't help it. Alzheimer's is worse than hell. Poor Grandpa. Fifty-five years of marriage, and now he is so alone. 'Who'd have ever thought it would come to this,' he says with quiet, heavy despair.

Soon she won't remember any of us. But when last she saw you and me, her eyes lit up, and she said, too loudly, but warmly, 'Well, well, here come two of my very favourite people.'

A while back, Grandma gave me two T-shirts from her track days, sixty years ago now. They are soft, gently faded. I wear them sometimes.

Lost

THE GIRL, FIVE YEARS OLD, and her Oma leave the bright red and white kitchen to go for a walk under the autumn sun. The wind is alive, rushing through leaves on the trees and in the streets with a sound like distant white water. Massive silver maples line the gravel road, their branches reaching together in the sky overhead. The little girl tries to fall into step with her Oma, but she soon gives up. Her Oma is not a tall woman, but her steps are steady, deliberate. She does not stroll. The little girl skips ahead then lags behind to wade through leaf-filled ditches. Far ahead is a ditch heaped to overflowing and she runs faster and faster, leaps, tumbles, and laughs. Dives down into the pile until she is buried. Hidden, she thinks. She is a leaf pile now, orange overalls and yellow hair blending with the birch and oak leaves.

I can still smell the earthy, moist warmth of that decaying foliage. I breathe in the memory as best I can.

Oma stops to pluck the leaf bits and green inchworms from her granddaughter's hair and clothes. They have reached the corner where they should turn, but today Oma continues. 'Where are we going?' the little girl wants to know. Oma is silent. It is an adventure, the little girl thinks.

Do you remember that day I practically begged for a sister? OK, I guess I did that more than once, didn't I, but there is one day in particular I am thinking of. We were driving home from swimming lessons in the rusty red Cougar. I was already in trouble, because I had left a white crayon on the black leather seat in the sun. The radio was on, or at least we could hear bits of music through the hiss and crackle of reception. Then the music ended, and was replaced by a voice. "Today's Child" waiting for adoption, I heard, was a girl, six years old…oh, maybe it was a boy. Or an older girl. I don't remember. Didn't really matter at the time.

I strained forward against the safety belt and turned up the volume. The voice swelled, filling the air between us until I felt myself pushed up against the door. You took a deep breath and held it. Oh no, I thought, now I'm in for it.

But when you looked at me, there was no anger in your face. Only this startling sadness, almost pain, that I didn't understand.

You turned the radio off. Never said a word.

"IN THE FALL DA HOAM, after the first frost, we made wine," Oma says. Apple peels are scattered on the counter and at our feet in crimson rings. Oma's knife deftly circles the fresh McIntoshes we are using to make applesauce. I struggle to keep up without slicing a thumb. The kitchen has the tangy, sweet smell of an orchard.

"In the garden behind the house," Oma says, "we had fruit trees, nit, all kinds. Apples and pears, plums, cherries…allerhampt hamma kopt, everything we had. One hundred trees or more. And all of the tree branches were covered in grapevines. They were growing up the back of the barn, too, and they would hang down so heavy with fruit. And we took those grapes, and we stomped on them in big vats. Oh, it was fun. Such a fun time hamma kopt, every year. Our feet and legs stained purple-red, and the sweet grape juice squished up between our toes." She laughs.

I try to imagine Oma without her bulky brown nylons on, without her shapeless Oma-shift dresses. Did she wear pants rolled up to the knee to do the stomping? Oma in pants. What a thought.

"And animals hamma kopt, too. Rauss we had, two sometimes three horses. Four cows to milk, and usually two young ones and two calves. And we had chickens, and geese, and dogs and cats. And pigs.

"Die Lynche, the young horse, came into the house to be fed. We had a Rigo, too, and Mitzi. Rigo we had to use blinders on, because he came back from the war afraid of everything. And Lynche, Lynche was funny. She always went into the kitchen. We had stairs, eight, and she went up them so nicely, and into the kitchen, where we gave her bread, from the table. She took it, turned around, and went back out. Once she got stuck between the table and the wall and she smashed a windowpane trying to turn around. The glass shattered and she jumped straight up and sent the lamp swinging. Then she stood there with her nostrils quivering, looking at me with her big eyes. She knew it was her last kitchen visit. After that, we fed her through the window. The cows had names, too, but I don't remember them."

I have to laugh. When Oma speaks of the farm she lived on during her marriage, and especially the animals, she can talk forever.

"And the *Sau* pig, her name was Linnie. When I went to the next village, to the market, she would walk with me, like a dog, *nit*. There weren't really cars, and when a wagon came, I would call to her, and she would wait with me by the side of the road. That mother Sau was special. What a *Sau*! She had twelve or thirteen piglets every year, and such nice ones. When she had them, usually in *Januar oder Februar,* I would sit with her in the stall, and when each baby came out we took it quickly, wrapped it up, the little one, and took it into the kitchen. And there we had a big basket that we put them in and covered them up so they would be warm. So they wouldn't die, *nit*. Until the last came. That last one we left for her. Then the next day we put them back in one at a time until she had all twelve. And she lay down, and they all went to drink. If there were thirteen I would have to feed the last one from a bottle. It was so nice.

"I still feel sorry for her. When the Russians came, we took her with us when we fled to the mountain. And when the Russians came there, they thought she was so big, so fat, *nit,* and they cut her open. They sliced her Bauch open and saw she was full of babies. Oh, I felt so sorry for her, really, she was so good."

We never did remove that melted white crayon stain, did we? You were going out with that Dieter guy at the time, or was it Atho...he was around for a while, too. I particularly hated the one guy, though, because he would always pinch my cheeks and poke my stomach and call me plump. A really chummy guy. Trying to win brownie points with you. Do you know why your six-year-old was afraid to go to the doctor? She thought he might put her on a diet.

I don't remember when I stopped petitioning for a sister. Must have been around the time you married Alexander. Must have, because by the time I was ten, something in me had decided it was too late.

I was terrible, wasn't I, when you told me. I remember sitting on the sheepskin rug in your bedroom, burrowing my toes into the soft fur. I knew something was up. Sat on my hands so I wouldn't pick my nails. You and Alexander looked down from the bed you were sitting on.

"We're going on a visit to Germany this summer," said Alexander.

"And," you said carefully, "I can finally give you what you've always wanted."

A horse, I thought, I'm getting a horse!

But then, "Mommy's going to have a baby."

My face turned red as though I'd been slapped. Then it scrunched up and I cried and blubbered like the world was coming to an end. Oh, I was a mess. Must have been awful to watch. Babies are ugly, and boring, and smelly, I told you. Did I? I don't know that I said anything. But I was angry, and frightened. I didn't want to share.

In the weeks that followed, I wished and wished it weren't true. And you knew, I'm sure.

"AND ALWAYS IN THE FALL I had my children," Oma says. She lifts the lid of the pot where the apple slices are boiling and fishes one out with a ladle. "Frank was born in October. The day he was born I went to work at the factory in the morning as usual. Then I knew it was time, so I got on my bike and rode home, and got the midwife. There was no one home, everyone was still working in the fields, *nit*, and then he was born. We didn't go to the doctor when we were pregnant. Not like here where they go every month, we didn't have this. Pregnancy is not a sickness." Oma passes me the boiled slice to test. "Done?"

I nod, enjoying the sweetness.

"I was twenty," she continues. "Married at eighteen, and so it was. And then after two years, in '34, the *Mädl* was born, the girl who died. And then I went to Budapest to work…"

"What girl?"

"She was sick—a blue baby. And then I went to Budapest to work, and then in '35 I went back home, and in '36, in September, Rudi was born." In one swift motion Oma dumps the apples into the metal colander. She takes the masher and begins to pound.

I look at Oma, perplexed. It's the first I've heard of this child. "Oma, what was her name?"

"Her name? Maria."

I see a tiny, blue baby. Blue hair, blue lips. I cannot see her cry, or move, even. A doll. And I see Oma, sitting by the basket in the kitchen, alone. Touching a cheek, an arm, making sure the soft blue skin is still warm.

"How long did she live?"

"Oh, three months, maybe four. Maybe not so long."

I search my brain for remnants of biology class understanding. A blue baby. The tragedy of different blood types. In the confusion of birth, the mother's body launches an attack on what it identifies as a foreign body. The most unnatural rejection. My fault? thinks the mother. Dare she love this child? For how long does she hold onto her hope?

I see Oma waking in the early hours of the morning. The fire has gone out, and she stumbles through the near darkness to stir the coals. Suddenly she feels the stillness, the unnatural stillness in the room. Before she reaches the basket, she knows.

When Franz awakens, he finds her sitting on the edge of the bed with the tiny, stiff bundle in her arms. He folds himself around her, but she does not look at him. Already she is gently wrapping her child into a soft silence. Tucking her into a hidden, private place that no one can disturb.

"And then the factory in town closed, and I went with the others to the factory in Budapest for a year to work."

"But, Oma, how could you leave? Why?"

"*Hah,* we needed the money," she replies calmly.

"But my Opa was the richest farmer, wasn't he?"

"*Ja,* but I had nothing. I was a poor girl, *nit,* and I had to earn so we could buy my mother-in-law out. She lived with us, and she hated me, so I went."

"But, Oma, didn't you miss everyone? Frank was only a little boy," I say.

"My brother and sister-in-law helped, and we had a stable *knecht*. They didn't need me, so I left."

They didn't need me, she says, so matter-of-fact. Isn't it logical? No, Oma, it's not. You boarded a train that took you hundreds of kilometres away. Away from a little boy scarcely out of diapers, and from a husband who did love you. And from a fresh grave, shoebox size, under the linden tree in the churchyard.

There is a stone marker in the churchyard. Or is it a wooden cross? I wonder, could you still find the spot, is it still there?

And so we went to Germany that summer. The trip is a blur. Is it that way for you, too? Alexander's mother presented us with a brilliant bowl of fresh cherries when we arrived. After that I only remember leaning over the toilet for hours, for days, willing myself to be sick. The overpowering smell of cherries and toilet water and vomit. So sick, sick, sick

And then you...all of that blood. I saw it on the bed, and being flushed down the drain in a swirl of startling crimson. And then you were gone, to the hospital, and I emptied my insides into that toilet bowl over and over. You were empty again, too. I'm so sorry.

THE LITTLE GIRL AND HER OMA are walking far, much farther that they have before. They walk through the tunnel under the roaring Queen Elizabeth Way. The ground trembles when transport trucks rumble over their heads, and the little girl holds her Oma's hand tightly. Then they are back on the quiet streets of an unknown neighbourhood. The little girl's pockets are stuffed with red leaves. In her hand she clutches wilting goldenrod and blue chicory. Oma turns with deliberate steps down an almost hidden alleyway behind the houses. The little girl sees a rabbit vanish into a row of tall cedars. Her eyes go wide, her mouth forms an *O*. At the end of the cedars is a clearing. There, Oma stops.

It is a cemetery. A Serious Place, the little girl observes as she wanders the neat rows. She runs her hands over the smooth stones, tracing the carved letters with her fingertips. Some of the stones are flat, flush with the earth. She joins her Oma at one of these flat stones. They clear away the leaves, push back the grass growing over its edges.

This is your brother, her Oma says quietly.

You wanted four children, two boys and two girls. When you were preg-nant that first time, with the boy, the world was beautiful. Aunt Heather has shown me your letters from those months. They are filled with excite-ment, anticipation, and simple details. Yellow you chose for the baby's room, with rainbow curtains and blue carpets. What did my aunt think of Montessori? Of cloth diapers? You were considering whether or not to go back to work after your maternity leave.

Then there was the infection. Bladder, I think. You are so vague about all of this. A premature birth. Complications. They whisked him away to the ICU immediately. Didn't even let you hold him. Tubes, monitors, and glass were placed between you and the child from whom you had never been separated. Aching, swollen breasts. Did you ever nurse him? Did you touch him? After a week, he died.

I cannot imagine the pain. But I cannot imagine it ever entirely leaving you, either. Oma must have visited you in the hospital. Was it then that she taught you the silence? Or is it something you inherited?

I've always known about my older brother. He is not a secret but we never speak of him. There is a difference; to keep a secret, you must hold it in your thoughts so that it won't slip out.

MY BROTHER, THINKS THE LITTLE GIRL. Oh. I have a brother. She is not as surprised as one might imagine. She must have been intro-duced to her father in the same way some years before. What is on the stone? David, his name is David. David Taylor? Or did he have a middle name? There is a little angel, perhaps, or a saying. "And God said let the little children come unto me…" No. The date: 1974. Must be. Just the one date? Or does it say, "After one week"? A year before the little girl's birth.

She squats down and peers more closely at the stone. There is a column of ants crossing the corner, and she blocks their route with her thumb.

When the little girl looks up, she sees her Oma's cheeks are lined with tears. Who are you crying for, Oma?

I don't know where that little cemetery is anymore. Perhaps if I walked those streets, I could find the alleyway. Tell me, who clears away the leaves? Who keeps grass and earth from swallowing the stone completely?

These lost ones. You don't want to unearth the memories, I know. But will you take me there?

Fathers

I GREW UP IN THE HOUSE my father built. Well, he didn't actually build the whole thing. Just gutted it and reconstructed it from within: tore out walls, moved doorways, added bigger windows, insulation, wiring, floors. But he left the original radiant water heating system. Miles of copper piping wind through the floors and walls so that in the winter the house gurgles and creaks as though it were alive.

One of the first Algonquin Park rangers set the foundation in 1946. The stairs leading to the basement have their corners lopped off to save wood — war stairs. The backyard, surrounded by the picket fence my parents put up, is filled with the ferns, trilliums, even trees the ranger brought down from the park. The ferns, high as my waist, form a luxuriant mass of green in the summer. Oma collects them in the fall when they are dry to help her arthritis. In the late sixties the ranger fell off a ladder into these ferns and died.

I was conceived the night my parents moved into the house, so the story goes. They couldn't find the keys, so my father had to break in through the basement window. After stuffing the window frame with newspapers, they sat together on the floor of the master bedroom in the dark. The first thing we need, my father said into the echoing space, is a bed.

Some nine months later, a jaundiced baby with black hair was born into their world of hammering and drilling and sawing. My mother set my basket on the low window ledge in their bedroom, and the hammering and drilling and sawing continued, the sounds competing now with a blaring radio. I slept.

It was a hot spring, a hot summer in 1975, and they worked up in the bedroom with almost nothing on, my mother says. One day she realized that all the neighbours could quite readily look in. The first things she sewed for the house were heavy, cream-coloured curtains.

The first thing my father made for the house was a bed. It was a very simple bed, really only a box of dark wood with a low headboard and no footboard so the featherbed drapes over on three sides. A good bed for taking flying leaps onto.

"MY FATHER, HE COULD DO ANYTHING," says Onkel Frank. "With his hands, he could do anything, you name it." He has just come in from fixing the gate in our crumbling picket fence. His woolly red and black checked coat is flecked with white paint. Oma has insisted he drink something warm before he goes home, so he has settled into a kitchen chair. I go to the neat white cupboards that my father made and fetch my uncle a coffee mug. He cups the steaming mug between rough, chapped hands. I have asked him what he remembers about his father, my Opa.

Oma joins in. "He could weave so beautifully, little baskets, big baskets. Wash baskets. Even baby cradles," she says, bringing a plate loaded with fresh apple strudel to the table.

Whenever I take Oma shopping she examines each wicker article and criticises it harshly. Look at these sloppy ends, she says in disgust, Your Opa's were much better than these pieces of garbage.

"Where did he learn it?" I ask.

"*Hah,* I don't know where he learned it. He saw it and he could do it," Frank says, spreading his hands.

"So that's where you got it from."

"*Ja,* it's true," he agrees without arrogance. "I see something, I can do it and improve it. Let's face it." This is true. He has fixed many things at our house over the years. Never pretty, but very functional. And the things he has designed are quite amazing: deluxe paddleboats with padded seats and tiny motors, various gadgets for Tante Frances to use in the kitchen. And those yellow hydraulic extension ladders used to work on power lines are his design.

"My dad had a great workshop. Beautiful. We had our machinery in there, and all of his tools, and a black potbelly stove for heat in the winter. I liked to help him. It smelled so good in the winter in there with the fire and the leather harnesses he was repairing." He closes his eyes and breathes deeply. For a fleeting instant I can see the boy sitting on a stool beside his father, diligently oiling leather pieces with a rag.

"Our father made all our toys, too. I remember my dad once made me a sled. Hid it for weeks, then gave it to me at Christmas. There was this big hill we used to go down, and we took that sled right away, Rudi and I, and we went so fast we couldn't get out and we hit a tree dead centre. And the sled just split, right down the middle. Oh, it was beautiful, all made out of wood, no nail in it, nothing. We took it home and stood it up, and Dad said, 'What did you do to it?' Then he touched it and it fell apart." Oma and Frank are laughing. I look from one to the other, but they seem to have forgotten me.

"And?" I ask Frank.

"And what?"

"What did he do?"

"*Ha,* he fixed it of course."

MY STEPFATHER, ALEXANDER, tried hard to leave Germany behind and become a Canadian cowboy. It was quite an obsession, especially when he first came. His hero was John Wayne. You can always tell it's him, I learned, because he carries his gun low and way back on his belt, almost on his butt. Alexander had the boots, the Wranglers, the Stetson. As long as he kept his mouth shut he looked the part all right. Alexander, the German cowboy. And I, his faithful sidekick.

I lived for those Western riding lessons he and I took together in rain and sleet and cold at that stable out on Bronte Road. My mother would look out at the weather and pronounce us crazy. Oma predicted darkly that we would ruin all of our joints and our lungs if we persisted in this stupidity. This only made Alexander set his jaw and pull on his boots.

There is a photo of Alexander on a horse, on a little hill off the trail. One hand is in the pocket of his jean jacket, the other holds the reins and rests casually on the saddle horn; he sits as though his life has been spent in the saddle. With his wiry frame clothed in denim and faded plaid, stubble beard and bright eyes glinting from beneath his hat brim he looks like the Marlboro Man. Oddball, his mount in the photo is a striking Paint horse with one blue eye and one brown. That horse was his favourite. Oddball could just fly if you let him. And we did. Sunday afternoons along the ridge above Sixteen Mile Creek. I can still hear the rushing water, the wind in the leaves, the hoofbeats on the dirt track. Holding on tightly to the saddle horn and ducking the whipping branches as my horse rushed anxiously after Oddball, I thought it was all absolutely wonderful.

"WHEN I THINK OF THE THINGS my dad did," Frank says, "he was so advanced, he was so far ahead of the other people in the town it wasn't even funny. You haven't seen anything here like what we had. Normally the animals would stand in the wet, but not in my father's stables. In the horse stables, and the cow stables, the water and the shit went into a main channel and disappeared underneath into big tanks. The same was with the pigs. It was all his idea. But the horses were his passion. That's where you got it from, Laura."

The summer before, Frank visited me at the stable where I worked. His face froze when he found me happily ankle-deep in manure. Slowly he shook his head. "I never would've thought it," he said when he could speak again, *"Erika's* daughter."

"He was a *Kreisbau Führer,* master farmer for the whole area," Frank continues. "Everything came to Binder to try first. He was the first to have fields with this special clover, for example. He cut it four times a year it grew so fast."

"But we had nothing modern," Oma interjects. "No running water or anything. Hot water we heated in a big tank above the stove. Frank, do you remember the hot bricks? In the winter we warmed bricks by the fire, wrapped them in rags and brought them to bed. You were always coming to me with blisters on your feet in the morning, do you remember?"

Frank is nodding, smiling into his coffee.

Oma leans toward me. "But your Opa, he *hat geschmugelt,"* she says in a half-whisper, letting the final soft syllable roll around her mouth, savouring the illicitness. I am not sure if this is a German word, or whether she has stolen it from English.

"From Burgenland down. Machines. He had someone who bought the stuff and smuggled it down. No one was allowed to know where it was coming from, or it would be taken and he would be punished. We had a new plough, an *Az*, and a machine to make cider.

"Otherwise," Oma continues, "we had nothing modern. In 1937 they came from the government and we had a vote in the village to decide if we wanted electricity. Half of the people said no. They said, 'What would we need that for'?"

THEY SAY I HAVE JOHN'S EYES. My mother's nose, my father's eyes. "You can always fix it some day," my mother has said of the nose.

John was a striking man. Nice teeth, dark hair with a roguish curl to it across his forehead. He liked to carry me around on his hip and to hold me above his head like I was flying. Apparently I liked this.

He wanted to build me a doll's house, my mother says, and to show me how to build model airplanes.

That last bit about the airplanes is pure conjecture. But I would have been interested. And I would have gone camping, and swimming and skating with him. We are a lot alike, I know it.

There is a series of three photographs of us together. Handsome man holding black-haired baby over his head, on his chest, face next to face. Both are smiling.

Is it possible to miss someone you never knew?

ALEXANDER AND I SPENT A LOT OF TIME in the basement making things. My mother had never cleaned out my father's workshop, and it was cluttered with stuff a creative mind could find useful. We made little trees out of the coloured wires inside telephone cables, or out of fine copper wires from the heating system. We glued seashells onto wooden plaques in abstract designs. We built a horse of scrap wood that would have been big enough for an adult to sit on if we'd ever finished it. We made papier mâché mountains with secret passages in them. And at the end Alexander got into wood carving. There is a sign hanging above the bedroom door that he carved out for my mother. On it in deep, solid letters is one word: Peace.

Once we wove a basket. Oma came down and stood in the doorway, watching us. She watched Alexander pushing the mass of fibres into a bucket of water to soak. Some of the dry straws were snapping and Oma came over to help. "Not like this," she said, reaching for the bucket. Alexander moved it away. "Just leave it alone, Oma," he said curtly, "we know what we're doing."

Oma really does know how, I wanted to say, but I didn't. Just kept fiddling with the unwieldy basket frame Alexander had put together. Oma stood there a moment longer, then turned and went back upstairs without a word.

I don't remember the two of them ever exchanging more than necessary words. Come to think of it, in those years with Alexander, I didn't speak to her much either. She was the worrier, the one who turned a disapproving eye on many of his exploits. Best not to ask at all if you are anticipating a "no," I reasoned; I had to regard Oma as The Law if I was to ride with my new hero.

Last time I was home I asked Oma what she remembered about Alexander. "*Ha*," she said, "what is there to remember? He went to work, he came home, he ate. He wasn't home much. That's all."

Not what I remember.

But when I asked about my father, her eyes filled and she shook her head. "There are things it is better not to think about, not to talk about," she said. But for how long, Oma? You can talk endlessly about the events of fifty years ago. Is that how long *my* mother will make me wait? There is so much I want to know.

MY MOTHER WAS GOOD about leaving us to play in the workshop. She would come down when we called her to admire our creations. Sometimes she would sit quietly and watch as I helped Alexander glue or plane or sand. He always had a pencil tucked behind his ear, and a little silver tape measure clipped to the belt of his ratty blue jeans, which my mother threatened to throw out but never did. I can still see the toothpick that would always be bobbing between his lips like a skimpy cigarette as he worked; he was trying earnestly to quit.

On top of the shelves of nails and screws there was an old radio. Paint-splattered and banged up, it would only play one station, he told me. So in 1985 I could sing the top twenty Country and Western hits by heart. Randy Travis, The Nitty Gritty Dirt Band, all of it.

YEARS LATER, MY MOTHER AND I were sifting through the clutter in a brave attempt at organizing the workroom. Dust billowed, curls of wood shavings cascaded to the floor as we uncovered paintbrushes with bristles dried solid, jars of faded seashells, Popsicle sticks and other useful junk.

"Out with it, out, out," my mother proclaimed, as she ruthlessly filled garbage bags to bulky overflowing. I watched in dismay as the comfortable, familiar mess was transformed into ordinary order. "We need some music in here," she said, and before I could warn her that it was stuck on a lousy station, she reached up and turned on the old radio.

There was, of course, nothing wrong with that radio. The tuner moved smoothly through the frequencies. I shook my head and laughed and cried and somehow couldn't explain.

"DID YOU WANT TO RUN THE FARM someday?" I ask Onkel Frank.

"Oh, heck, yes," Frank says with his mouth full of strudel. "Oh, my dad, when I think..." He shakes his head slowly. "He was good. Already when I was ten he treated me like an adult. Not like here, where kids get coddled until they are thirty. He taught me how to do everything, to use all his tools, all about the crops and the animals. He would say, 'Franzl, you have to learn. You have to learn responsibility. Because,' he said, 'someday you will take my place, and I want to be proud of you.'

"This was all before he had to go to the war." I hear wonder, reverence, regret in his voice. I suddenly wish I could have known my Opa. This is a new thought. These details, these everyday memories are making him real for the first time.

"And when I think of the fruit trees we had, *mein Gott, na*. You name it, we had apple trees from everywhere you can think of, my dad brought in. They came on the railway. From Hungary, Austria, even from America, you name it. There must have been twenty varieties, a couple of hundred trees. You could look at any angle down the rows and you only saw one tree. That's how accurately he planted them. I don't know what we did with all those apples."

"*I woas ah nit*," I don't know either, Oma says, shrugging. She shoves another piece of strudel toward her son. "But he loved those trees."

"*Ja*, he was so involved with *veredeln* — what you call it again? Plant breeding? Yah. When I was seven or eight years old, I went into the woods, to the wild cherry trees and, I'll never forget, I took a branch from there. Behind the work shed he had such nice McIntoshes. So I went up into the middle of a tree, a big tree, and I cut a branch out, and I grafted the wild cherry on there. I was so proud when it grew in the spring, and the next year, it bloomed white in the middle of the red. There was this tree of red blossoms with one branch of white. My dad, oh, was he mad." Frank is laughing again. The sound is more a child's giggle, only rougher and deep.

"*Ja*, you were a real *Lausbub*. Into everything. But he was proud of you, that you learned from him," Oma says.

"He was?" Frank exclaims.

"*Ha ja*, when he told me about that tree, he laughed and said how much you'd learned."

ALEXANDER TAUGHT ME how to lose. I remember card game marathons at the cottage. Snowy evenings before the fire playing endless variations of a German Crazy Eights. And my mother would get so frustrated by losing streaks, accusing Alexander and me of collaborating against her. She was so funny about it, throwing her cards down dramatically, declaring she wouldn't play with the likes of us again.

I'd lose too, of course. "Ha, ha, too bad," he'd tease. "Let's play again." And I would. Until Alexander came, I'd never lost at anything. Oma let me win every game we ever played. And I couldn't handle teasing at all. Especially not from my mother's boyfriends who thought they were being "good" with me. So I guess you could say Alexander toughened me up, gave me backbone. Taught me how to play the game.

"MY DAD WOULD DO ANYTHING for me," says Frank. "That was my dad."

"He helped everyone," Oma adds. "When someone came and said, *Du,* Binder, drive me there and fetch this for me, he left everything and helped. He did everything. And despite this they always *haben geschimpft,* always criticized."

"Because he was rich?"

"Because he was rich. They said *geizige* Binder. But he wasn't stingy. He would leave his work and do theirs, then would do his own. He often said, 'If you need help, just ask.'"

They fall silent. The coffee is finished. Frank starts to rise from the table, but I want to know more—they can't stop now. I slide one more piece of strudel onto his plate. "Was he a talker?" I ask.

"No," says Frank, sitting down again. "He didn't talk much. He was, I think, more like me."

"Who?" Oma asks, confused.

"Dad. He was more like me."

Oma looks at her son and grins. "He didn't talk half as much as you."

"But his temperament was more like mine," Frank persists, ignoring our laughter. "When he got mad, he hit, like how I used to do. He hit me when he was mad."

"But he didn't get mad often," Oma says quickly. "Almost never."

Frank said, "The only time he always got mad was with grandma, his stepmother. She always said, 'You let Frank get away with everything,' and she would go on and on and on, needling him, and finally he would get so mad that since he couldn't hit her I got it."

"*Ja,*" Oma says, chuckling. "That's true. But you usually deserved it."

I AM OUT ON THE DRIVEWAY with my bike. Alexander and I have been arguing about something stupid, I don't remember what, over lunch hour. My mother is flying, Oma is at bingo. I have ten minutes before the bell rings to be at school. He is standing at the window. I am still mad and my anger pulls my tongue out, just a tiny bit, and points it at him. In a flash he is out on the driveway. He grabs my arm and my bike crashes onto the gravel. His eyes are furious and he slaps me across the mouth. Then he goes back inside. I pick up my bike, see the scratches in the red paint. I pedal madly away to school. I am mostly concerned that kids at school will notice my puffy face and red eyes.

Alexander must have talked to my mother because she sat me down some days later and explained that I must never show disrespect, that he takes this very personally. So after that, I would stick my tongue out between my teeth and keep my lips closed.

"FRANZL, DO YOU REMEMBER Dad's Christmas trees?" Oma asks her son.

"Oh, *ja*. Christmas was so nice at home. I think it was nicer than here."

"Was there snow?" I ask.

"Oh, heck, we always had a metre of snow."

"*Ja,* snow we had enough of," says Oma. "When me and Mitzi went to the factory, we walked on top of the snow, *kreutz und quer sind wir gangen.* It was so frozen, over the fields. We could walk over everything. Even the fences were buried. Sometimes we still tried to bike, but we would get up on one side and fall off the other. It was funny."

Frank turns to me. "At Christmas we had a tree, our father made it."

I raise an eyebrow.

"*Ja,* he did," Frank says. "We had so many Christmas trees in our woodlot, and he was so good with them, tending and pruning all the trees. Not like the others who just let them all grow cramped and crooked. So before Christmas he would go out and clip out branches from different trees, one from here and there. Then he took a pole and drilled holes in it and wrapped it with green material. And he stuck those branches into it."

"It was a perfect Christmas tree. So beautiful." Oma wipes her eyes. "And no one could ever tell that it wasn't a real tree. Imagine, every year he made us one that was special."

Frank is crying too. I am embarrassed, and rise to clear the table.

I AM IN MY SNOWSUIT pulling the red toboggan with the saw in it through the neat rows of pine and spruce. We are going Christmas tree hunting, just Alexander and I. Going far, past all the other people at the tree farm until we are making fresh tracks. Just white snow and green trees and blue skies in front of us. We are explorers, searching for the perfect tree. Alexander pulls me in the sled when I get tired, and we ride down the hills together, the saw in my lap. I can hear the whisper of snow compacting beneath us as we slide.

Finally we choose the tree. More because the sun is setting and we are tired than because it is closer to perfection than the others. I cry as it falls. Alexander does not laugh at me. We have killed it. I count the rings on the sap-bleeding stump. It is my age. Each year I think this.

At home it is my responsibility to water the tree every day. I crawl under the branches on my elbows with the watering can, needles collecting in my hair, until I reach the trunk. I am at the heart of the Christmas smell, and I breathe it in. Then I talk to the tree, tell it that it is the most beautiful Christmas tree ever. And I gather some of the needles to keep, each year, in carefully labelled jars, so there is a memorial to each of the trees that dies. I have always been one for remembering things.

NOW MY MOTHER IS TALKING of selling the house my father built. The new owners would probably gut it again, change everything. And I think this would be good. My mother should have moved a long time ago.

I can say this from my safe distance; when I am within its familiar, comfortable rooms I cannot imagine it any other way. I love the place. And I hate it. Now when I go home, I feel its sadness. Such a heavy, heavy space. It exhausts me to be there. Doing anything, even sleeping, takes more effort in it. I lie in bed for ages listening to the walls gurgling and moaning and can't sleep. I need to be away from the house to think clearly about anything. But particularly to think about all that has happened within it.

Deportation

*I*T IS THE FINAL EVENING of our visit at the cottage. Frank and I are
standing on the dock, watching the last sunset colours fade from
the surface of the lake. The air is cold but completely still; the water is
a perfect mirror. A fish jumps. Ripples move through the reflected trees,
the thin lines of birch white against the inky blackness of the firs.

"Will you look at that," Frank exclaims. "Just look at that. Could
there be any place more beautiful in the whole world?"

I agree.

"I have everything I could ever want," he says. "Up here, nobody
bothers me. Only people we want to have bothering us. And we
have all the birds and the deer and everybody, it's just beautiful." He
shakes his head in wonder. "Just think what we would have missed
if we'd stayed over there."

I leave Frank on the dock and climb back up the steep steps to the
porch where Oma and Frances are sitting in comfortable silence.

"So you're glad you came to Canada?" I ask them both.

"Oh, *ja,*" Frances says immediately.

"In Yugoslavia, where Frances is from," says Oma, *"die Partisanen,*
the communists were murdering whole households of Germans in
their beds."

"We had to go," Frances says. "But that's another story."

"They came with their oxen and wagons," Oma says, "endless
caravans came along the road through Jakobshof. They were fleeing
for their lives."

Frances nods but stays silent.

I settle into a chair and wrap my jacket tightly against the deep-
ening chill.

"For us it was different," Oma says. "It was spring again, 1946. We went to work in the fields, ploughing and planting everything again. We had no horses, *nit*, so Frank and me, we pulled the plough. And when we found bombs in the fields, we put big sticks in the ground to mark them. *Kartoffeln,* and the *Weizen,* everything we planted.

"And then in '46, in April, we got a notice telling us we were going to be deported. It didn't say to where. It just told us when we had to leave, and what we were allowed to bring. It said that we could take only thirty kilos. Sixty pounds we were allowed to take, per person."

"How much is that?" I ask.

"Not much at all, but we didn't have anything anyways. Because the Russians took everything, all the clothes, everything, except what we had on."

"They took your clothes, too?"

"*Alles, alles,* everything they could. And what the Russians didn't take, our people took, the ones who turned communist. So we packed what we had."

"What did you take?"

"*Ha,* all the bedclothes we had, and what clothes we had. A pot to cook in. Ladles. A good knife. And food, but we didn't have much. Bread I packed, and I made an *Einbren* of dried egg for soup *unterwegs,* for the journey, *nit.* We hoped we could boil hot water somewhere and then add the Einbren, and that's what we would eat."

I think of the photo of Opa on Oma's wall, of their wedding picture, and the photo of Opa posing proudly with one of his horses. I think of the photo of Oma's mother in her American finery, of Oma and her sisters laughing in 1920s flapper dresses, and I imagine Oma sliding these prints from their frames and carefully tucking them between the sheets in her suitcase. Lighter squares on the dirty wall mark their absence. For once she does not feel compelled to clean.

"Did they tell you where you were going?" I ask.

"No, no. Ask Frank. He's still convinced we were headed for Siberia. The labour camps in Siberia. And it's true, lots of Germans ended up there, from Poland, from Czechoslovakia."

"For being German?"

"*Ha ja,* that's the language we all spoke, *nit.* When Hitler lost the war, the winners said all the Germans must be deported back to Germany. From everywhere. From Yugoslavia, from Hungary, from everywhere. But we weren't German, and Germans didn't want us.

"So then they came for us. It was just getting light when they came, the Hungarian soldiers and the Russian officers with their wagons. I looked around one time more, at our house with the hole in it and the newspapers in the blown-out windows. I looked at the kitchen garden by the linden tree, where the peas were about to bloom already, and the yellow *Löwenzahn,* the dandelions, were everywhere. I could smell the blossoms on the fruit trees in the orchard, and from the purple *Flieder* hedge. And somewhere a cock was crowing, but only half-crowing, I can hear it still. *Ja,* he crowed like he had no hens, like he was unsure if day had come.

"And then I went inside one more time, to make sure the fire in the kitchen was out. Stupid. What did it matter? But I had to check. From the old table where we used to sit, everyone together, I wiped some stray breadcrumbs into my hand. Then I left quickly, and closed the doors.

"The soldiers lifted Rudi, your mother and me up on the wagon with the rest of the people, and Frank climbed on with the bags. And then they drove us away to Unterradling. I remember seeing trails of smoke from cooking fires out in the fields by the river when we left Jakobshof. I thought at first they were gypsies, and that was strange, because we hadn't seen much of them since the war came. Later we learned that there were Hungarian families camped out there, waiting to move into our houses.

"They drove us to the train station in Unterradling. We spent the whole day there, in a field outside the station, until night, until it got dark. Soldiers watched so that no one could leave. We asked them where we were going, but they wouldn't say. I don't think they knew."

"How many people were there?" I ask.

"The whole village. And not just us, from all the villages. From Radling, from Unterradling, from Fidisch, all the German speakers, the Austrians, *nit.* There must have been a hundred people, more than that.

"It was so hot in the field, and your mother, she was getting sick. She had been immunized the day before, and it was making her sick. Milli and Resi stayed with us the whole day. We just sat together. It was good to be together like that. There was nothing to say. We thought we might never see each other again. They didn't have to leave."

"Why not?"

"Because they were Hungarian citizens. They married Hungarians, *nit*."

"What were you?"

"Me? I was an Austrian. I belonged to Burgenland province in Austria, because my father and my husband were from there.

"And so Milli and Resi brought us food that day. And they gave us more to take, too. Wine they gave me, five litres. So we would have something *unterwegs*.

"And there was a long train standing there all day, a train that transports animals. I thought we were going to sleep in the field, because our train wasn't there yet. But then, when it was dark, they started herding us into the *Viehwagonen,* the animal cars. I couldn't believe it. We were all so stunned, *nit,* that no one complained. When we were all in, they shut the doors and locked them. In an animal transport we went."

"How long were you on the train?"

"Oh, I don't know how long. *Eine Ewigkeit.*" Forever.

"Was it dark?"

"Oh, *ja*, we went at night, *wie die Räuber.* Like the thieves. We didn't know where we were going. It was completely *finster,* pitch black even in the day. Not one window or anything. And so closed up, we had no air. In our car we were…the Schmied family, they were three children, five, seven, eight in all," Oma adds with her fingers. "And then there was me with mine, we were four, so twelve. And then there was my Onkel and Tante, they were five. Twelve and five are seventeen. And *die* Schandar-mam, with Ella who was so sick, makes nineteen. And then there was *die* Steidel-Mitzi, with her two daughters, that makes nineteen, twenty, oh, I don't know how many."

"All in one car?"

"All in one car. And then there was *die* Krowotin, with her two boys.

Her husband was forced to enlist with my husband. And we were all in together, and we couldn't sleep, we couldn't do…anything. And you couldn't get out if you had to pee or something, nothing. We had a big bucket, and we all peed in it. Two, three days we were in the train, I think. *Unterwegs* they stopped, and we could get some air. But only after we got over the border…at Hegeschalem, I think. We must have gone north. And then we went up…I don't know where all we went. We didn't know where we were going. And in Salzburg they stopped again.

"But before that they stopped only once where we could get out. The train stopped out in the fields, there were no houses or anything. In no-man's land. There we got out and washed ourselves in a little *Bach* that ran by the tracks. And we got water, and made a fire, and there I cooked the soup. We were all dirty and stinking together, and we washed ourselves and hung our clothes up on the bushes in the wind to dry. We were there a couple of hours, I don't know how long.

"And your mother, she was so sick. I thought she would die *unterwegs*. She wasn't moving at all, and the immunization site was so *eitrig,* pus and blood and everything, and her hand was so swollen, I thought she was going to die. There was a doctor, but he couldn't help her, he had nothing with him, *nit.*

"And then we continued, and when we got to…now, where did we go…before we got to Salzburg. *Ja,* when we went over the border the train pulled into a prison camp. And there they made us line up in two lines, the women and the men, in front of a big barracks. Inside, we had to undress, everything, and they sprayed us with some white stuff, like flour it was. All white. They sprayed us, and our clothes. Because they said we had so many lice, that we were covered in lice."

"Did you have lice?"

"Some did, yes. Then we had to go through this big room that was a shower, where they washed all the white stuff off. The water was cold, and Erika was still so feverish in my arms, *nit,* I thought she would die. We spent one or two days there, until they had done everyone. They made me take off my wedding ring when we went in there. I never got it back."

Frances and I exchange a glance. She shivers.

"Were these still Russians?" I ask.

"Oh no, they were Germans. They were Hungarians until the Austrian border, then we were taken over by the Germans. And that's why we were all de-liced. The Germans said they wouldn't take us as we were.

"From there we went to Linz, where we stopped again. There we got a bit to eat. Finally in Linz there was a doctor. He examined Erika, and gave me a cream, and I applied it and she slowly got better.

"And there in Linz he was waiting for us, my husband. There he came to us. He was still a prisoner of war. When we had learned that we were to be deported, I wrote to him. Somehow he found out I was on the transport and he was waiting for us. They had released the old ones whose families were being deported. It was a long, long time that we hadn't seen each other. Since Resi and I visited him in Gmunden, in '45."

"How was he?" I ask.

"How he was? He looked really good. He already had cancer, but he didn't know, no one knew. But they let him go with us.

"And so we went again in the train until we got to Bayern. We were transferred to Wasseralfingen, a military camp in Bayern somewhere. There was nothing there, just barracks, and they had straw inside to sleep on. We were there perhaps eight days. There we were given food, and then we could decide where we wanted to be taken. We were asked if we wanted to stay in Wasseralfingen, or if we wanted to go to Württemberg. We didn't know where Württemberg was, or what Bayern was, or anything. And so we asked the people there. They said it would be better in Württemberg, because there were more factories there, more work. But they just wanted to convince us not to stay and take away their jobs, *nit*. And so we gathered together, those from Jakobshof, we all let ourselves be signed up for Württemberg. That's why so many are still there. The Schmieds, the Seinberger, the Urwer, the Krowert, *die* Jaust, the whole town, except for the ones who came to Canada, to the States. We were many.

"And so we were taken to Bietigheim in Württemberg, where there was another big camp."

"On the same train?"

"Oh, yes. And then we spent two or three weeks in the camp in Bietigheim. There we were already given food. But *nix gscheits,* no proper meals. One week we had lentils, and one week we had beans for the whole week."

"But, Oma, they probably didn't have any food either."

"They had, but the men that were in charge of doling food out for the *Flüchtlinge,* they took all the good stuff home. We weren't even given milk for the children. The milk was completely blue. They put just a little milk in, the rest was water. The milk they took home for their families, and fed their sows."

"How do you know that?"

"Because the people saw. Worse than the Russians, some of those Germans were." Oma shakes her head in disgust.

"*Ja,* and in Bietigheim your mother, she was still sick, *nit,* but there she was crying, all the time crying. We were over two hundred people in that room, and when a child cries in the night, no one can sleep. But wine we had still. Milli had given us five litres of wine, *nit,* for my husband, but he didn't drink much. By now he was so sick, *nit.* He said just give it to Erika so she will be quiet, so the people can sleep. So when she cried, I gave her drops of wine. In Bietigheim she drank all that wine, and she slept.

"And so we got to Pleidelsheim. And then in '58 we came to Canada."

Frank climbs the last of steps and joins us on the porch. He sits down heavily.

"You telling Laura how we were deported?" he asks.

Oma nods.

Frances looks at him in dismay. "Frank, we were just about to go inside," she says, standing up.

Frank doesn't seem to hear. "When they threw us out," he says, "they just came and took us away. Into the wagons, you know, like you see the Jews, they talk about the Jews all the time, we were no different."

"Except they weren't planning to kill you," I say.

"They didn't want to kill the Jews. You know who killed the Jews?

The English, the Americans, the Canadians killed the Jews. The English were the most at fault. They wanted to send them all to England. But England didn't want them. The Americans didn't want them."

I take a deep breath. "But Frank, the Germans shouldn't have sent them away in the first place!"

"I know, that was stupid. But now the Americans want to play the big guy, the good guy. But in war, everyone is bad, everyone. And what happened with us, everybody just forgot. We were going to Siberia, to labour camps. That was our destination."

"Are you sure?"

"Oh, *ja*, that's exactly where. Oh, *ja*." Frank is nodding vigorously. "The train went Russia way. Then, for some reason, they changed their mind and let us go to Germany."

"Why?"

"*Ha*, maybe they already had enough going that way."

"They sent you away just because you were Germans?"

"We weren't even Germans! We were *Burgenländer*, Austrians. And the Hungarians didn't want us, they wanted us outta there." He pounds his fist into his thigh. "They were cattle cars, we were standing in there no different than the Jews, and they locked us in, and we were going east to Russia. That's what I remember."

I see Frank, a boy of thirteen, boarding the train that will take him far from everything he has ever known. He sees his mother, all of the adults, filing aboard in silent submission. Their helplessness overwhelms him, and he wants to shout at them, 'No! Stop!' But he knows he should be afraid, and he is. When the doors slide shut he tries the latch and finds it locked. The train begins to roll.

Frances goes to her husband and gently lays her hand on his arm. "But now we are here."

Oma is looking out into the trees, nodding.

It is almost dark. From across the lake a wolf cries.

Frank gets to his feet and opens the door.

"*Ja*," he says. "Now we are here. Thank God."

I Remember

OMA AND I ARE MAKING SCHNITZEL in the cold light of a February afternoon. A stack of slippery pink chicken breasts sits on the counter beside a bowl of whipped egg. Beside that is a mound of flour, then a mound of breadcrumbs. A deep pan of oil is sizzling faintly on the stove. Oma is pounding the chicken flat with a mallet, then I am doing the dunking and breading. I try not to touch the raw flesh if I can help it.

Oma laughs at my squeamishness, and when I have buried the chicken in the breadcrumbs she takes her hands and presses down on top of mine. *"So must du's machen,"* she instructs. Like this. The buried meat feels surprisingly soft and pleasant beneath my fingers.

"Your Opa loved it when I made him *Schnitzel*," she says, smiling. "When we were in the Baraken, in Germany, I was so happy when I could get chicken for him. Pork or beef we couldn't dream of."

I pull my hands out of the flour. "He was in Pleidelsheim with you?"

"Ha ja, my *Mann* met us in Linz, on the way to Germany. *Ja,* he came with us in the train from Linz all the way to Pleidelsheim."

"So he didn't die at the refugee camp in Bietigheim." This is half a statement, half a question. I tuck wisps of hair behind my ears, forgetting my flour-covered fingers. My mother had told me he'd died there, I'm sure.

"Oh no, not there. The war he survived."

How odd that my mother does not know this. Or maybe I have just remembered it wrong. Yes, probably. But when I told my mother I was learning about Opa she did smile ruefully and said I probably already knew more than she did.

"So how was he when you got to Pleidelsheim?"

"How was he? He still looked really good on the outside." She lowers the first of the *Schnitzel* into the oil and the pan erupts into violent spluttering, sending searing drops of oil toward unprotected skin. Oma reaches calmly across the pan and reduces the heat.

"So when we got to Pleidelsheim, again we were put in a camp. Out in the forest, a kilometre out of town, there was a prison camp where they had kept soldiers. There were four, five long barracks, and there in those barracks we were put. We had to live there for almost a year. When we arrived the wires were still up, four different kinds of wires. Coils of barbed wire were lying around that children and dogs got cut by and tangled up in.

"There were four families in a room of this size; each one had its own little corner. No privacy anywhere, not to cook, not even to wash up." She takes the last of the uncoated chicken and pounds it with forceful strokes.

"And we had no firewood," Oma continues. "We were living in a forest, trees all around, but we could take nothing. We got up in the night to go wood chopping. Brought it in by night and chopped it up inside, in the barracks. Your Onkel Frank almost got shot one night. The farmer who owned the woods where the camp was almost killed him. Almost shot *mein Sohn* for gathering firewood."

I wait while the muted thud of mallet striking flesh continues. The chicken is very flat.

"Why were they so awful to you?" I ask.

"*Ha,* they said, 'Here come the Hungarian gypsies. And they steal,' they said, they steal, so the people locked everything up, they were so afraid we would steal. 'And they don't work,' they said, 'they want only to take.' This is what they thought of us, before we even arrived." She picks up the pulverized meat and dumps it into the flour. "That's why I've never liked Germans."

"But weren't the Germans required by law to take in the refugees?" This is what I have learned in school.

"*A va!*" she snorts. "The mayor, *der woar so einer,* he gave us nothing. We were supposed to get wood, and this and that, but they gave us nothing. Even the stores where we brought our ration cards, only one would serve us. The others all said they were out even when we could see they weren't. You know Herr Kozel? His father owned one of the stores. He was one of the worst."

Yes, I know Herr Kozel, a retired senior executive of Lufthansa. When I asked Herr Kozel about his father's store, he told me how his father and brothers came back from the war as thin as stick drawings, of how there was never enough for anyone; Oma knows only one side of the story. Everyone was living in hell, Herr Kozel said, everyone.

It is his cottage up in the Haliburton Highlands that we look after during the winter when he and his wife are in Germany. The Kozels have been good friends of our family for years now. Oma always treats them like minor royalty when they are in town.

"We got to Pleidelsheim in June, July maybe," Oma says, "and the men, they could go to work on the roads, in the fields. But my *Mann*, he was already sick. Because in the camp we didn't get anything proper to eat, and because he already had the cancer. He got thinner every day. He got as thin as a stick. And he couldn't go to work anymore." She pokes at the frying *Schnitzel* with a fork. "And then. *Ja*, and then he couldn't eat."

I was raised by my mother and grandmother. How often have I said this? "Just call me Mrs. Taylor," you say, leaving off the hyphen and the Kummer. How often have I heard you say this to my friends? It's easier. So much easier than having to explain. Yes, I reply to the inevitable question, my mother remarried. Yes, he died too. And then I watch as they suddenly do not know where to look and the conversation loses its colour. It's just a bit of death, we think, annoyed by the reaction. Get over it. But it is not that easy to get over.

You say you don't need to go back, that you don't see the point in talking about it, about them. These men whose lives were, for a time, so intimately linked to your own. You say that you just aren't the type who needs to remember, to talk. Maybe that's true.

Of course there are places in your memory to which you cannot yet return. I have those places too. "This isn't the time to think of these things," you reason, "I want to be able to sleep tonight." You say this as though thinking that there will be a time when you can settle down in a corner of your life and grieve. But what if that time never comes? What is not thinking about the past doing to you now?

I would not be writing this if I didn't think the silence is hurting you, hurting us. I am one of those who do need to remember. More than that: I feel we owe it to ourselves, and to them, not to forget. Maybe this is stupid. Maybe.

December fifteenth, 1975. You get up quietly, not wishing to wake John. Some time later you call him for breakfast, get no response, go to him . . .

I can't do this. I cannot go there with you. I cannot go into that room. Not yet. Maybe never.

I know you tried to revive him. I know you called the ambulance. I know you ran outside screaming for help. These things I know from the doctor down the street who heard your screams and came running. And could do nothing.

I cannot go into that room with you. But I was there, eight months old, sleeping in the corner. Did I cry?

A virus attacked his heart, you told me when I was little, and one day he just didn't wake up. Some kind of freak heart attack. The coroner's report was inconclusive, but deemed it "natural." When is death at twenty-eight ever natural? His pilot's insurance covered him for everything except a natural death. But he left us one material gift: the house. His death cleared the mortgage. The word mortgage comes from the French, "death pledge."

So I grew up in my father's house.

His death is the key, isn't it? You fell apart after John died, I've been told. You fell into so many pieces that when you could finally gather them up, many were lost. So of course you couldn't afford to let that happen again. Of course. But I am afraid, too. Afraid that, in trying so hard to block the bad memories, you've blocked the good ones, too. So we still come up short on pieces.

"DID YOU KNOW OPA had cancer?"

"No," Oma replies. "He had pain, *nit*, but the doctor, he wouldn't look at him. Because we were *Flüchtlinge*." The *Schnitzel* in the pan is a deep golden-brown. Oma spears it with a fork and lets the excess oil drip back into the pan.

"How long was he sick?" I ask, handing her the next piece.

"Oh, a long time. *Ja,* and when we went again to the doctor they couldn't help him. At home he couldn't even eat anymore. I made him anything he wanted. But he couldn't eat it. One day I begged a farmer for a chicken, I begged him for just a piece, because we had nothing. And when my *Mann* saw I was making it for him, he was so happy. But then he ate a forkful and everything came up." Her face floods with tears and I don't know where to look. She has taken me into so many dark places. But never have I seen her like this. I go to the window and stare into the bright grey sky. The oil hisses loudly as it attacks breadcrumbs and meat.

Oma clears her throat. "So we took him to the doctor again, *nit.*" Her voice has levelled to the point of flatness. The words flow like a chant. "And because he was so bad, and had such pain, the doctor sent us to the hospital in Marbach. So he went to Marbach, and there they examined him, and saw that he had cancer. Stomach cancer. He was there eight days, then they operated. Well not operated, just opened up. And they saw that the stomach and lungs and heart and kidneys and everything was already full of cancer; they couldn't help him any more. They cut him open to see, then closed him up again. And on the ninth day he died."

THE KOZELS' COTTAGE, March 1988. He can't get out of bed. Lying there, twisting back and forth. Clutching at the sheets. Come, Alexander, please get up, please. Yes, yes I'll be right there, he says. Or some incoherent words. Or sometimes nothing. Just silence that isn't silent. And his face. Something is wrong with his face. His left eye clenched shut, his cheek pulled up, pulling his lips on that side up, up. A smile and a snarl and neither. The muscles never relaxing. I can hear the dog whining in the corner.

And then the ambulance comes. I am outside now, holding the dog. The sun is glaring off the snow. The snow is high, up to my chest. I watch the attendants struggle down our shovelled path from the road with the stretcher. Watch them carrying him out, all wrapped up. I cannot see him for the snow.

I REMEMBER SITTING IN CLASS on the day of Alexander's surgery, watching the clock over the blackboard. Imagining what was happening in the operating room.

I see them shave his head until it is smooth and shines like polished stone. The first incisions are neat and clean and bloodless, peeling back his forehead like the skin from a peach. Then the piercing whine of the saw biting bone.

"Laura, are you all right?" It is Mrs. Mapstone, my Grade Seven teacher. "I was calling you. You look so pale, hon."

I tell her someone in my family is going in for surgery. She assures me that everything will be fine. Surgery is so routine nowadays.

I could have told her then that when they remove a brain tumour, the procedure is still very imprecise. They have no detailed maps of the brain; there are no guarantees. No way to tell how much good will be scooped out with the bad. No way to know what mental functioning will be affected. No guarantees.

I liked Mrs. Mapstone. Sometimes I even wished she were my mother. But on the day of the surgery I smiled and nodded at her reassurance and pretended to concentrate on long division. I never told her about Alexander. No one at school ever knew.

The headaches started in the summer of 1987. Around the time Alexander quit his job managing that restaurant because he was bored with it, and because he couldn't stand his female boss, right? He wanted to get into computers.

I remember riding with him in the forest by Sixteen Mile Creek the day he told me we were getting a Dalmatian puppy. I was so excited that I didn't mind not letting the horses run that day because the pounding gait hurt his head.

You two started arguing a lot that summer. All I remember about a short trip to Prince Edward Island that July was being completely mortified at a bed-and-breakfast when you had a rip-roaring row in the bedroom. The elderly woman there was nice to me. Took me by the hand into the garden to play with the snails.

By that autumn he would often fall asleep on the couch with the puppy curled in his lap, snow on the TV screen. It was becoming too much effort to go up to bed. You read this as apathy.

The family doctor treated Alexander for a stomach ulcer, right? Never thought to look for the cause of headaches in his head. I can't believe this man is still your doctor, and Oma's too. I guess after everything you figure one is as useless as the next.

All winter it dragged on, the headaches, the fights, until one day that red X appeared on the calendar in September. Eight months you were giving him to shape up or else.

"I should have realized," you said afterward. "I should have known, yes, I should have known there was something very wrong. That he wasn't the person I married." There was anguish, even guilt in your voice. As if someone else, someone more...what? Someone more sensitive? Someone more aware would have thought, "Gee, maybe my husband has a brain tumour"?

I have a confession to make that is much worse. In a journal entry from that summer, I tried to order, as objectively as possible, the people in my life that I loved. I tried to decide whom, if someone in the family had to die, I could handle losing if I had to. Is this what most twelve-year-olds write about? And I decided—I still have this journal, it is there in purple ink—that if someone in the family had to die, it would have to be Alexander.

"AND THEN WHEN I WANTED to bury Opa," says Oma, "I couldn't get a coffin. So then I went at six in the morning, it was a Sunday—*i vergiss es Heut now nit*—in January, the seventeenth of January. *Ja*, I still remember so well. There was no snow, it was so beautiful, and the moon shone so beautifully, and where the sun was coming the sky was *rosa*. And everything was sleeping still. Nothing moving, no wind even.

"I got up in the morning at six. And Erika, she was still little, I took her to the neighbours, to Frau Modock, who looked after her. Rudi and Frank would come later—the funeral was supposed to be at eleven. And so I got up at six, and walked into the village to wake Frau Schmidt, she was a *Totenfrau,* one who was a *toten beschauer*… she took care of everything with his body, *nit.* She was a German, but she was good to us. I told her that I had no coffin, and the funeral was at eleven. The mayor was supposed to give over a coffin for him, but he would not. In Marbach they wouldn't give me one either. So Frau Schmidt got dressed and then we went through the village from one *Tischler* to the next. And no one would give me a coffin."

"Why not?"

"Because I was a *Flüchtling, nit,* and they were so *flüchtlingsfeind.* One wouldn't even open the door when we knocked. One said it would be a waste of his wood. And of course I had no money either.

"It was getting later and later. Frau Schmidt, she said she knew one other, she said. 'Let's go there.' The woman at this last place was a widow, also; her husband had died that year, too. And she had one coffin. Take it take it, she said, I don't need it anymore. But it was only boards quickly nailed together, and still all white, the wood. She had two *Gsellen,* apprentices of her husband, and she woke them up, and they quickly painted that coffin. Brown. And we had to wait a while until it dried, and she had a wagon that we put the coffin onto, and we had to pull it ourselves all the way out to the hospital. Empty it wasn't that heavy.

"By eleven it was quite dry, and then we buried him. And afterwards I was alone with the children."

Once, you told me this story. This is how I remember you telling it:

"I went to him in the ICU *after the surgery and waited for the anaesthetic to wear off. I sat beside him and held his hand, the one not connected to IV drips and all those monitors. No one could tell me how he would be when he woke up—if he'd be able to see, hear, or speak. Or if he would wake up at all. Even with all of those fancy monitors, no one knew.*

"Then he did stir and open his eyes. They slowly focused on my face, and I said, 'Hello, Alexander.' He looked up at me with this puzzled wonder. 'Am I married to you?' he asked me. And when I said yes, he gave me this huge smile, and went back to sleep."

I remember you recounting this with most tender humour.

145

I WAS VISITING WHEN THE NURSE CAME in to undo his turban of bandages and remove some stitches. As she unwound the layers of gauze, Alexander chattered to us, unconcerned. Very much alive. He even knew us. Well, most of the time. Maybe, I thought, this will be OK. Maybe, I thought, there will be a miracle.

Then the last gauze fell away and I saw the scars. A Frankenstein roadmap of stitches running in both directions across his head, red and swollen. I watched the nurse pull the little threads out of his head, one at a time. The staples will come out later, she informed us cheerfully. I could watch, and my stomach stayed put, but with each thread I felt further away from this man on the bed who was and was not Alexander. When I kissed him good-bye I was surprised that his cheek was soft and warm.

I remember you coming home after the meeting with the surgeon. More new words: malignant, frontal lobe, short-term memory centre. He told you point-blank that Alexander had maybe six weeks, that he would never leave the hospital.

And you cried. You cried. The only time I can remember, through all of this. We stood there on the sheepskin rug in front of the bed my father made and we held each other for a long time.

BUT HE DIDN'T DIE. He came home. By summer he was even driving again. Except someone always had to be with him, because he would get lost in streets he'd driven a thousand times. It was kind of funny, having to tell him when to turn onto our street. "Is this where we live?" he'd ask as we drove under the great arching silver maples, delighted over and over again.

We even travelled that summer. Down to my Grandpa Taylor's winter place in Florida. I remember my mother letting Alexander go by himself from the beach to the apartment to get something. A good two hours later we finally found him, lost in the elevator. He couldn't remember the apartment number, or why he was in an elevator, or why he was in beach clothes.

By then I did not know him at all. Nor did I want to.

AND THEN IT WAS FALL AGAIN. September 1988. The day marked with the red *X* came and went without comment.

I can't remember much of my thirteenth year. School, yes. Grade eight. Mrs. Mapstone again. And books, I lived in so many books that year. What else…the class trip to Quebec City where all the boys bought cigarettes and alcohol and knives. Suffering heat exhaustion at a track meet. Being teased by the boys about not shaving my legs: "Your father was an ape, ha ha." Finding a new best friend. Yeah, I remember lots. But at home…what went on? I moved through the house with a waxed paper wall between myself and everyone else. The year is still mostly a blank. Punctuated by images, images I push away with all my strength, but which will not stay away.

The worst one took place at the cottage, during March break 1989. Alexander is standing in front of the mustard-yellow fridge, confused about something. He is wearing one of his stupid hats that look like cloth lampshades. He wrinkles his forehead and the train-track scars bunch up above his eyebrow. I can see tufts of new hair like down, stuck to his scalp. His jaw is slack and he juts his head forward like a turtle. "Heh?" he says. "Heh?" His eyes are void of everything but bewilderment.

I hate him in this image. I hate that I remember it. Why do I have to remember this? And why can I only remember his grin when I have the help of a photo?

For that year I'd see him in the morning before school, and then again for a bit when I came home. As soon as I walked in my mother would say, "Don't forget to say hello to Alexander." He was almost always sitting in bed under the covers, propped up with pillows, the TV on. The tall yellow lamp made his skin appear even sallower than it was, and cast strange shadows beneath his eyes.

We must have talked. But about what? What do you say to some-one you know will not, cannot remember five, even three minutes later? I did not age for him. I think he had me stuck at about ten years old. He was never in a bad mood. Not angry, not sad, nothing. He could not hold onto information long enough to reach those emotions. Quite a blissful state, I suppose. No wonder people get addicted to drugs that take you there. In almost two years of chemo, radiation, immobility, he never realized how sick he was, what was happening to him. Life was only ever in the present tense. "Today, I don't know," he'd say, "I'm not feeling too good today. I'm sure I'll be better tomorrow."

But more than once I found him with his hands in his pants, his eyes half closed, moaning and sucking air. He was obviously still feeling, still living in ways I didn't think about then. Now I wonder. What *did* he think about? What kind of hellish circles was he trapped in when he could make no new memories? He could never reach any new conclusions; every emotion, thought, or worry was frozen forever. Or so I imagine.

But his oldest memories remained intact. And he must have lived in them. Close to the end, he would insist on saying grace before each meal. The man I knew as highly irreverent would sit at the table with his eyes shut and his hands together and pray the prayers from his altar-boy years, crossing himself solemnly. Was he reliving the memory? Or was there more to this rediscovered piety? Did some part of his brain register his condition?

You knew. More than any of us, you knew what was happening to him. I retreated behind my waxed-paper shield. I don't know where Oma was through all of this. So you were always alone in the hell you lived with him.

The weeks and months of radiation treatments and the chemo. I do remember the little targets on his head, red marker Xs with circles around them to line up the rays. It was harder and harder to get him out of bed as the weeks passed because the treatment made him so tired. And every morning you had to explain all over again why he had to get up…I heard, as though from a great distance, you trying as I got ready for school in the mornings. Coaxing, cajoling, enticing him to get up. Helping him into clothes. Always gentle, never raising your voice when you would leave for a minute and return to find him curled up under the covers again. I don't remember you getting frustrated; your patience seemed infinite.

Each time he was back in hospital, you'd be there every day. I'd come, too, when you asked me. I felt alien, always, walking those corridors thick with hospital smell. The neurology wing was always silent, as though all breath was permanently suspended. We celebrated my fourteenth birthday in the Princess Margaret downtown. Do you remember bringing in the cake? We both sat down on his bed and spilled crumbs everywhere. It was almost fun.

Alexander often shared rooms with breathing bodies: beings with little functioning besides lungs and heart; tubes for food, others for excrement. I tried not to look at them, but there is one man I remember. His face was young, probably Alexander's age, not quite forty. It was a beautiful face, with thick red eyebrows and many laugh lines. But the lower jaw was stuck open, frozen in silent, perpetual scream. There were cards stuck to the walls, lining the cupboards, everywhere. Dear Mr. Johnston, said a banner, please get well soon. To the greatest teacher in the world. We miss you.

It was too much. Too much for me. I'm so sorry I left you on your own with all of this. That I couldn't help you.

I REMEMBER SITTING in the kitchen eating with Oma and Alexander in the grey light of early spring, eating soup with *Knödeln*. All of us are gazing out the window. I am watching crows scratch at the grey-green earth in the backyard. Soup spoons clink gently against china like muted chimes. Alexander suddenly gets up and lurches to the bathroom off the kitchen. The toilet bowl amplifies his retching.

Oma looks at me. Her eyes are dark wells of an old pain. *"Saw ist es dein Grossvater auch gangen am Ende."* Your Opa, he couldn't keep anything down either at the end.

I try to ignore what she has said.

IT IS A MORNING LIKE ANY OTHER. I am on my knees shoving books, pens, and lunch into my rucksack, rushing to make the school bus as usual. Tante Christine, Alexander's sister, is here from Germany for a visit. My mother and aunt are helping Alexander out of bed. He is teetering on stick legs, grasping for support. He lurches around the bed as they try to hold him up, to balance him. They are making encouraging noises, soothing noises. I only half see this as I have learned to only half see everything that goes on in our house. But the stick legs do shock me. I haven't seen him out of bed in weeks. His pyjama pants are slipping. There is nothing holding them up but bone. No muscles, no fat, just bone. I think of the nurse in Emergency a year and a half earlier asking if he was a marathon runner because he had such a sleek figure, such incredible leg muscles. No, a soccer player and a rider, I'd answered proudly. And now, so very, very weak.

Somehow they get him to the bathroom. I hear them shifting, banging around. "Say good-bye to Alexander before you go," my mother says through the slats in the door. She is taking him to the hospital again. They are going to continue the search for the primary tumour. They have established that the one in his brain is secondary. So why is it so damned difficult to locate the first? There are only so many cells in a body. Surely…well, whatever, I think. So I say 'bye through the slats in the door, 'bye Alexander. And he says 'bye, too, I think. From the toilet where the two women are helping him pee.

This will be the last time I see him.

You told me this once, Mom. You took me to this place once, and this is how I remember what you said:

"I am sitting by his bed, staring past the white curtains, past the white hospital room walls. He is sleeping. Unconscious? He has been slipping in and out for five days. Whenever the delirium breaks, he sees me, and he puckers his lips. Kiss me. But he is never really there. Just a flash of himself before the cancer's face returns, the one I have learned to recognize, yes, but never to accept.

Now he is sleeping. Unconscious? And I sit, numb. I am thinking in a foggy way about hope. How it is never lost, even when it should be. That the human brain punishes itself with optimism.

My gaze breaks, and I shiver. I feel a change in the room, as though someone has dimmed the lights slightly. The white walls look suddenly grey. The monitors circling his bed are still blinking, austere. Their little red lights are like so many blind eyes watching. I reach out to stroke his arm. And then I see his fingernails. They are turning blue. Grey-blue.

The nurse I shout for is professional but kind as she checks the monitors. The red eyes are blinking faster now. And my own heart is racing, my head feels light. I pull that stupid hope, every last bit of it, up and into my words until they are full and trembling with it. 'Please do something. Isn't there anything you can do?' The nurse looks at Alexander. My words hang in the air for what feels like forever. 'No,' the nurse says gently, 'there is nothing more we can do.' And then she leaves, closing the door.

And I sit beside him, holding his hand. It is turning blue. I stroke his forehead, his chest. I love you, it's OK, I say. It's OK it's OK, I love you, I say, until he is gone. And I am alone in the room."

I can count on my fingers the number of times Alexander's name has come up in the years since he died. It is as though he has been erased; a six-year blip that never really happened.

But don't tell me you don't live with it every day. Every morning you wake up in the bed my father made. The bed he died in. The bed Alexander spent two years dying in. What does this mean? I can't believe that you have blocked out the past so effectively that these material reminders hold no power. I can't believe this.

I think of Alexander when I am coiling rope or cord. I see him teaching me to mow the lawn, then to coil the electrical cord. He swings his arms in sweeping, rhythmic arcs, the cord collecting in his hand in neat loops. I think of him on the rare occasion that I am on Bronte road and see the subdivisions going up along Sixteen Mile Creek.

Otherwise, I don't think of him often. Weeks, sometimes months go by when I don't consciously think about all that has happened. But when I wake up in the morning beside my boyfriend, I hold my breath so I can hear his. I watch to make sure his chest is rising. It is a habit I cannot break.

"Those stones are these monuments they," I say, showing my mother the map.

"Looks like it. Why?"

"Those were all the Jewish stones. Brokstadpth," I characterized for them, sad alterations it have forgotten and recalled, too.

We sit in silence. My mother rubs the remains of humans silently. Despite the oppressive heat, she shivers.

"Come, let's get out of here."

In the uncomfortable, awkward, unfeeling silence that engulfs us by the time we reach our hotel room, I am giddy with the horrors we have seen. We sit together on the bed, comparing our hunger for flexibility, feeling silly and elated. My mother tries it out and angles it, and we congratulate ourselves on a long, exhilarating day.

THE NEXT MORNING, after touring the medieval fortress at Güssing, we are driving along the only route that narrowly winds between it and the border, searching for Kangaria, the village where Oma and her children weathered the later months of war. You are leaving into the lands considered road signs superstition.

"You go that way," my mother chants just after we pass around another crooked, unmarked intersection for what feels like the hundredth time. I search for a place to turn around. The road she has chosen leads us consistently upwards, growing more narrow as it climbs.

My mother looks down into the valley and shakes her head. "I'm telling you, if we go over the edge, that's it, we're dead. They'll never find us."

I groan. At every turn in these hills she sucks air sharply between clenched teeth and grips the door. This is becoming increasingly difficult to ignore.

When the road before us dwindles to a cow path, I turn the car around and stop. The land surrounding us is deeply rolling, with hills high enough to make my ears pop. Clusters of red-roofed houses are tucked into the folds of these hills like enchanted hamlets in a sunken novel. The gentle slopes are seeded with grapes or corn or

162

PART FOUR

Return

I PUSH THE WINDOW BLIND halfway up to watch the light-blue beginnings of the sunrise high over the Atlantic. My mother slips back into the seat beside me and clicks her safety belt on. She has been in the galley exchanging the latest gossip with the flight attendants.

"A year retired and I'm so behind," she says. With a sigh she makes her seat recline. "But it's so nice to be a passenger for a change."

I smile and let my eyes close. One week. I am about to spend a whole week travelling with my mother, alone with her for the first time in years. We are both brave.

We are flying to Munich, then on to Graz in Austria, then renting a car and heading for Oma's borderlands. I am going to do the driving, since I have driven in Europe before, and besides, I have a more intuitive sense of direction and I am calmer than she is.

This trip was my mother's idea. She phoned me up a few weeks ago and said, "Let's go to Hungary." In the whirr of busyness that followed, I had little time to let my excitement build.

I turn my head toward her. "So what made you decide we should do this?"

She closes the magazine she has been skimming, and considers.

"Well," she says, "do you remember the last visit? All that rain, and I can still see Oma just looking around and saying, *So, jetzt hab i alles gsehen. Jetzt kamma wieder gehn.* Now I've seen everything, we can go again. She was so nonchalant, so disinterested in the place. We never really got involved, not really. You know what I mean?"

I nod, and she continues. "So I guess I want to see the place I was born. To really see it." She studies her fingernails for a moment. "You know, I never really listened to the stories, not like you do. They were interesting, but they just never interested me. I don't know why."

Inside my camera case is tucked a map that Oma and I have constructed of Jakobshof and the surrounding towns. The school, the *Gasthaus,* and the bakery are on it, all the houses and who lived in each one. I have marked where the paths lead up into the forest to the church, to the communities in the hills, like Hausergraben and Jakobshofer Berg where Oma hid when the Russians came. The railway, the creek and the river are on it, as are the gardens and orchards and what they planted in them. The map grew and grew as Oma spoke, and I needed to add sheets of paper to follow her gestures of memory. It took six sheets taped together at their edges to draw Oma's world.

My mother is armed with a list of names of people to look up, dead and alive. There is an old woman in Unterradling named Julia Stern, a friend of Oma's from her youth. Go over the creek, say Oma's instructions, and before the cemetery in the old schoolhouse she will be. If she's still alive, that is. Oma says Julia is the last person who speaks German in all the towns.

Oma also wrote down the names of her father's relatives, the Schrei family, who came from Deutsch Minihof, another minuscule dot on the Austrian side of the map.

When I arrived at Pearson International in Toronto the day before, my mother came to meet me at the luggage carousels.

"I'm Austrian!" she announced.

I looked at her, confused. "Um, yes," I said. "Of course you are."

"But all these years I thought we were Donau Schwaben, those Germans like Tante Frances who had resettled in the East centuries ago, but I'm a Burgenländerin from Austria."

I was anxious to leave the airport, but the passion in her voice made me lower my backpack.

"I've done some reading," she continued, "and the border was only formally drawn in 1920. That's when Austria took over the province of Burgenland. But when they drew the border, some Austrian villages—Jakobshof, Oberradling, Unterradling, Fidisch—got stranded on the Hungarian side of the line." She shook her head, frowning.

"So actually they weren't German at all. They'd always been there. I think it's stupid that the Hungarians shipped them to Germany. Ridiculous. Absolutely ridiculous," she says, drawing out the word. "They could have just shipped them to Burgenland, three kilometres across the border. That's where all their relatives were, not in Germany. Ridiculous."

"Not their relatives," I corrected her. "Ours."

Now, breathing the dry, compressed air and trying to switch my thoughts into the German-mode I will need when we land, I'm curious again about my mother's sudden passion for history.

"So," I ask her, "why now?"

"Why now…" she murmurs, thinking. "I guess until now I've been too busy making a living, keeping food on the table, worrying about you. I've never had the time."

I feel my ears pop as the plane begins its descent.

I LIE ON THE BED IN THE GRAZ HOTEL watching a dubbed episode of *Cagney and Lacey,* waiting for my mother to finish getting ready. I look at my watch. What does she do that requires an hour and a half every morning? When she finally emerges from the bathroom I sigh loudly.

She ignores my impatience and looks critically at herself in the mirror. "Does this outfit look OK?"

She looks fantastic and I tell her so. The latest in three-quarter length summer pants and a sleek T-shirt emphasize her slight, still youthful figure. I see my own reflection beside hers and pull at my jean shorts, feeling dumpy, provincial. Damn it, how can she possibly still have this effect on me? I look into the suitcase and feel I have nothing to wear. Slump onto the bed.

"What's the matter with you?" my mother asks.

I feel like a teenager again, groaning that nothing fits.

"Don't be silly, Laura, you look just fine! Good, actually. I really don't understand how you can't see it yourself. Just ask your boyfriend, I've seen how he looks at you."

I laugh and haul myself off the bed. "I'm ready for breakfast."

It is chilly on the street leading into the old town where we will pick up the rental car. My mother shivers and turns into the nearest clothing store. I find her a cheap but stylish denim shirt with which she is extremely pleased. A few stores further down the cobbled street, we wander into a shoe store where she insists on buying me a new pair of sandals I look at, the latest style. I don't admit it, but I walk away in them feeling much better. Pathetic.

We pass a bookstore with a sidewalk sale in progress and I have to stop and look. My mother is already well down the street when I call to her. "Mom, come look at this."

She checks her watch, then humours me.

I have found a book on Hungarian cuisine. As we flip through the colourful pages of recipes and photos—five whole pages on paprika—I feel my mother grow tense.

"Will you look at this—a recipe for *Zwetschgenknödel!*" she breathes. "And *Kropfen* and *Gulasch* and *Krumpenkauch*. I don't believe it. Everything is in here. This is just what I've always looked for!"

"So now you're going to cook?" I ask.

"Sure, why not? The recipes are all here." My mother rushes into the store to pay for the book. I can't decide whether to be pleased or frustrated.

"Oma can teach you all of it," I say when she returns.

"Yes," she replies, "but here everything is written down for me. That's how I work."

We walk in silence, taking in the crooked streets, the uniformly preserved architecture of Austria's largest medieval city.

"Oma says I don't talk to her enough," my mother says, her tone helpless.

"Oh?" I say carefully.

"*Ja,* she complains that I have no time for her, I don't know what she wants."

"Maybe it's not about talking," I say. "Maybe it's about listening. Why don't you try cooking with her again?"

"We are trying," she says. "We even baked a *Gugelhupf* together last week and it was edible."

"That's good," I say, sounding as encouraging as I can.

158

"IT'S SO MUCH BIGGER than I'd expected," my mother says as we wander the streets of Heiligenkreutz, the Austrian border town that will be our base for the next few days. The sky is hazy with heat, and the pastel plaster colours of the many new houses going up give this landlocked place a Mediterranean feel. The yards we peer into are as full of fruit as Oma's stories tell: peach, plum, pear, apple, and apricot trees, grapevines winding up every fence and trellis. An old man waves to us from the ladder where he is picking cherries. Smoke rises from an American-style barbeque, and a young girl passes us on rollerblades. I'm surprised by the prosperity. The Hungarian border is only two kilometres down the road.

The next morning we join the line of vehicles waiting to cross into Hungary. We roll the windows down to alleviate the heat and are assailed by dense exhaust spewed by Eastern-block trucks. My mother coughs and I try to ignore my own rising nausea. The Hungarian border guards speak animatedly with my mother when they see in her Canadian passport that she was born in Jakobshof. They are disappointed when she says she cannot speak Hungarian, but she speaks enough with them to impress me thoroughly.

"Oma didn't teach you all that, did she?" I ask.

"Oh, no. I learned it long ago, from a Hungarian boyfriend," she replies.

I wait in vain for her to elaborate.

Not a kilometre from the pass control, the road bends to the left, carving through gentle green farmland and suddenly we are there, on the street of streets. A massive transport is bearing down on us, and I cannot decelerate. I see the sign for Jakabhaza and we are already zipping past the huddled houses. All I manage to glimpse are huge, gaudy letters proclaiming *Geld Wechsel* — "Money Change" — stencilled on the side of an old building.

"That's new," my mother comments, shifting in her seat.

And then we are through Jakobshof, and are hurtling toward Unterradling.

"What is that?" my mother exclaims. I take my eyes off the road long enough to see, on the otherwise empty slope to the left of the road, a new structure. It appears to be windowless, is black with hot-pink trim and surrounded by a large parking lot.

"What is *that?*" my mother repeats. And then, in a voice choked with disgust and disbelief, she reads the English sign.

"It's called "The Titty Twister.""

My mouth drops open. And then I find myself laughing. After a second, she joins me. What else can we do?

FROM OMA'S MAP we locate the little road just before Unterradling that leads up into the hills to the church. We drive past a short row of crumbling houses. Plaster is missing in chunks, revealing walls of tiny red bricks or, in what I take to be the oldest, a mixture of mud and straw. Through the dust we are churning up I catch glimpses of faces watching us from doorways, through heavy lace window curtains. Suspicious, probing faces. I keep my eyes on the road.

It winds up into the most beautiful deciduous forest I have ever seen. Massive beeches, their bark smooth as skin, arc their limbs over our path. The lush forest floor is flecked with sunlight. I slow the car to a crawl and roll down the window to let in the cooling moisture of the tree shade.

My mother laughs. "I could just leave you here, and you'd be happy, *gell?*"

We park at the base of the last climb to the church. Oma says that there were many houses right here by the church, a *Gasthaus* and even a school. I look into the thick forest and find nothing. No houses, no paths, not even a foundation poking out of the undergrowth. Of the community there is no trace.

As we walk toward the church, we pass a battered, overgrown sign indicating we are entering the border zone. Danger! It warns in both Hungarian and German.

St. Emmerichskirche rises out of the trees before us, its onion tower and yellow walls trembling in the heat like a northern mirage. The church where Oma was baptised, and my mother as well, sat abandoned in no man's land for fifty years. We stop outside to read the plaques explaining the restoration it underwent in 1992, accomplished with funds from Austrian, Hungarian and international sources. My mother examines the photos taken in 1990 before the restoration and shakes her head. "Senseless."

The church was a roofless, ruined shell. Trees were growing in the tower, their roots breaking through the plaster.

Inside the thick walls, I stand and read the sign hanging above the simple altar. It is written in both German and Hungarian: Faith knows no borders.

When I emerge from the church, my mother is in the trees, peering at something in the greenery. I join her and see that she has discovered the cemetery, or what remains of it. In the deep shade of the old linden and oaks there are maybe five stones still standing. The others are almost completely lost in the brambles and high grass. We walk among the stones, trying to decipher names, dates. All the names until 1946 are German. All are familiar, though none are family.

"There must be other cemeteries closer to the village," my mother comments.

I nod, clearing some weeds from a crumbling, illegible stone. A tiny angel with one wing adorns its top like a grounded bird.

"Do you think Oma's baby is buried here?" I ask.

She shrugs. "Perhaps. That was a terrible business."

"What do you know about it?" I ask, still absorbed by the once-delicate features of the little carving.

She hesitates. "Remember when you asked me to ask Oma about the poppies?"

"Yes?"

"Well, she told me they took the *Mohn* heads and boiled them, and fed the solution to the babies. So they would sleep when their mothers went to work in the fields."

I look up. "She never told me this."

"She said not to tell you because it was illegal, what they were doing." My mother pauses to reach down and brush the dirt from a plaque set flush with the earth. "So anyways, the baby girl was born very sick. But after a time Oma had to go back to work, and left the little one with her mother-in-law. She thinks that her mother-in-law gave the baby too much of this opiate, and that it killed her."

I let myself lean against one of the old lindens and close my eyes.

When I open them, my mother is already out of the trees. I pick my way slowly through the undergrowth, careful to avoid the stones. When I am with her again we start down the path behind the church. Red stakes in the ground every few metres mark the border and I stand for a moment with one foot in Austria, one in Hungary. There is an ancient linden tree growing right on that border line, its ponderous limbs swaying slightly in a breeze imperceptible to us on the ground.

"Reminds me of one of those family trees people draw," my mother says.

I nod absently.

"I'm sorry I was so terrible when you told me you were pregnant."

My mother keeps walking. "You were?"

"Yeah, don't you remember? I've felt ashamed about it ever since," I say, embarrassed now for having brought this up.

"You know," she says, "I really don't remember. So much happened right after, that I guess it just wasn't important."

"Oh," I murmur.

"Amazing how differently people remember the same thing, isn't it?" she observes, her tone light.

We turn and walk slowly back to the car.

ON THE WAY INTO UNTERRADLING to search for Julia Stern, my mother points to a pair of storks circling above the power lines. The spruce treetops on which they land bend under their weight. One throws its head back and starts clapping its beak. The noise reminds me of a drummer rapping his sticks together, and I peer up at the gangly, black-and-white bird in fascination.

My mother laughs. "Why did you think they were called *Klepperstorchs*?"

The heat seems to thicken as we walk. I look back anxiously toward the store where we have left the little red rental car; the theft insurance for Hungary is high. My mother jumps into the ditch each time a transport truck blasts past us, which happens every few seconds.

Unter- and Oberradling are now called just Roenoek.

"Oma says, *Über den Bach, vor dem Friethauf, im alten Schulhaus*," I recite Oma's directions. Over the creek, before the cemetery, in the old schoolhouse.

My mother looks around helplessly. "We'll never find her."

I hear running water, and point to a wavy line of reeds leading away from the road. "Look! This must be the creek."

My mother nods reluctantly. Soon we reach the rusty wrought-iron fence of the cemetery. I push on the gate and it opens. Here too, the graves are German until 1946. The rest are Hungarian. Except for one.

"Michael Stern," my mother reads, "1958." The pansies before the stone are freshly watered.

"Well, someone's still here," I reason.

We backtrack to the three possible houses between creek and cemetery. A large, middle-aged man in a stained white undershirt and tight Adidas track pants is watching our progress from a doorway. My mother approaches, managing to stay out of reach of the hungry-looking goats tied to stakes on the slim strip of grass between pavement and house. I smile and try to look friendly as I take in the cracked windows, the stinking rabbit cage and scruffy chickens. The man does not speak German, but when my mother says, Julia Stern, he smiles and points to a house two down. When he smiles, the teeth he still has are almost black. The people look like their houses: falling apart.

In contrast, the house he directs us to is neat and clean, with flowerbeds full of poppies and tall purple lupins. A tray of apple slices sits baking in the sun.

"That's more like it," my mother whispers to me.

We find Julia in the garage, resting beside a sack of apples. She is a little, solid woman with a sunburnt nose and bright white hair held back with a black headband lined with tiny plastic pearls. She is wearing a *Kleiderschurtz*, a housedress that could be Oma's, knee-high stockings that leave her knees bare, and black lace-up shoes. She does not seem surprised to see us.

"Who's this who has come to see me?" she asks, beaming. We introduce ourselves. Her eyes open wide and she clasps her hands.

"*So, die* Laura *lebt ah noch?*" she says with wonder.

"*Ja,* she's very much alive," my mother says. "Looking good, like you."

She runs a hand over her hair and laughs coquettishly. "*I bin mehr z'nichts. I han aber lang g'owbert.*" I'm not good for anything now, she says. But I worked a long time.

I blink. These are pure Oma-phrases rolling off her tongue. I can't believe my ears.

We sit in the cool garage and talk as though we have always known each other. Julia lives with her son and Hungarian daughter-in-law, who brings out a bowl of chips and a carton of orange juice. I comment on the beautiful poppies.

"I would offer you a *Mohnstrudel,*" Julia says, "but it is three days stale."

Her daughter-in-law speaks only Hungarian, but when she hears we are from Canada, she grins at us and says, "Scarborough. Richmond Hill. Maple leaf." My mother and I look at her, perplexed. Julia explains that she has a sister living there, just east of Toronto, and that she has even been to visit.

In less than ten minutes and with no prompting from us, Julia is talking about the war. She speaks of leaving for Yugoslavia with her five children when their house was bombed out, of finding the promised new house already occupied, of sleeping on people's floors for weeks, all in a row like matches in a pack. Of running out of food for themselves and their animals, and fording the swift Raba with the bridge out to return home.

"When we finally made it back," Julia says, "my littlest child, the girl, she saw her father waiting for us in the field and she couldn't wait. Down from the wagon she jumped and ran and ran to him, yelling Papi Papi Papi." She wipes at her eyes, shaking her head.

"*Du kannst es nit glauben was wir oalles mitgmacht haben.*" You can't believe what we went through, she says. Watching her, I think of Oma, of how happy she is when I come home. So many stories trapped in these very old people.

"And then after, Laura and everyone was deported. Everyone, everyone, was gone. It shouldn't have happened, I don't know why it happened. There's no one left, no one."

"Why did you get to stay?" I ask.

"*Ha,* my husband, he was a *Burgermeister,* a mayor, *nit,* and so it was." She waves vaguely. My mother and I exchange a glance. He had joined the communists.

"But it shouldn't have happened. My *Mann,* he died years ago. Now I am the only one left. But I'm not dead yet!" Her laughter is hollow.

I take photos, and my mother gives Julia fifty Deutschmarks, a present from Oma. She has to insist that Julia take it; apparently this is a lot of money.

After over two hours, she kisses our cheeks and sees us to the gate.

"Tell my Laura she should come back," she calls. "Tell her that we'll go dancing!"

She waves until we are out of sight.

OMA'S MAP IN HAND, we walk through Jakobshof. At each yard we pass, aggressive-sounding dogs leap at us from behind locked gates, and again I feel watched.

My mother points to a nondescript house. "Last time Oma said this was the school."

I align the map with the road and nod. From where we are standing, it is easy to see that the map Oma drew after almost sixty years is still accurate. We pass some houses and more dogs until beside us is a large plot of unused land, overgrown with pumpkin vines and sunflowers, rhubarb and all manner of wildflowers. I look at the map.

"It's the Big Garden!" I declare. "Behind the garden is the baker, and from there a path should lead into the forest to Hausergraben, Jakobshofer Berg and the church."

Sure enough, there is a path along the garden's edge. We follow it hesitantly until a house comes into view. Two young boys with a soccer ball look at us crookedly and disappear behind the house. A teenager is sitting with two women shelling walnuts in the shade of a massive wild rose bush. The young man speaks some German, and my mother shows him the map. When the women understand our quest, their closed faces bloom with smiles, and they offer us walnuts.

"Was this a bakery once?" my mother asks.

"Yes," they say, "yes, it was."

My mother smiles at me, triumphant. "And this path?" she points to the map. "Hausergraben? Jakobshofer Berg?"

They all study it closely. "No," says the teenager, "no path. Nothing in the forest." The women shake their heads. *"Nix da."* Nothing there.

I look at the women. They are my mother's age, perhaps older. Too young, I realize with a start. They are too young to remember anything.

My mother explains that we are from Canada. One woman smiles brightly. "Oakville!" she says, "Niagara Falls." She has a brother in Canada. My mother and I exchange a glance. Bizarre. Oakville is fifteen minutes from our home.

WE DECIDE TO SEE if there is anything left of the grand *Kastelln* where Oma worked as a child. There is a chicken farm in its place, but as we look up the driveway, a building at the back seems too old and elegant to be a part of it.

"The servant's quarters?" I suggest. We inch our way up the drive to see if there is anyone around to ask. Suddenly four dogs explode from behind the barn, barking like mad things. They surround us, and I talk to them. They aren't trying to bite, so I decide not to be afraid. I look up just in time to see a man stepping behind the barn. I know he has seen us, and I am annoyed.

"Let's just go," I say to my mother, who is bravely trying to befriend a bellowing bulldog.

When we turn to go, I see another man. He is standing in a shed not twenty feet away, watching. He still hasn't called off the dogs. I resist the urge to glare at him. My mother walks over and shows him the map. He shakes his head. No, nothing left.

ON THE WAY BACK TO THE CAR, we stop in front of the *Gasthaus* where Oma and her sisters used to hear music and dash across the road to join the dance. It is still a restaurant. And a convenience store. A neon sign proclaims "Open 24 hours."

I want to take pictures of a window in the house where Oma was born. This is the house, we realize in dismay, with the "Money Change" stencilled on the side wall. Just as I focus the camera on the red geraniums and flaking paint of the window, a face materializes within the frame, an angry woman's face. She shakes her finger threateningly and I lower my camera.

"So, you are taking pictures of the village," says an Austrian voice behind me. The restaurant owner is standing in his doorway with his hands on his hips.

"My mother was born in that house," my mother says quickly.

The man's posture softens and he beckons to the woman in Oma's house.

"You see," he explains, "when foreigners take pictures here, they usually are looking to buy; land is cheap. People here feel threatened."

It's not their land to sell, I want to say, whether they know it or not. Instead, I take a picture of the woman who lives in Oma's house. The Austrian — whose wife is Hungarian it turns out — has explained to the woman, and now she is standing with her fleshy arm around my mother, smiling. Again the rotting teeth.

On the way back to the car, my mother is quiet. She stops and looks back into the village. A transport rumbles past, blowing her hair across her face. "You know what Oma used to say when I was a teenager?" she says. "That if we'd stayed here, I'd be herding swine on some mountain."

IN ST. GOTTHARD WE STOP for coffee and ice cream in a little café on the main drag. It is a lifeless, uninteresting place, we decide after walking its empty streets. Maybe it is the heat. I count at least three dental clinics, their signs all in German.

"Cross-border convenience for Austrians," my mother comments dryly.

Across from us is the church, an imposing structure whose spire you can easily identify from the Austrian side of the border. Beside it is a row of stores in old buildings whose ornate façades are sorely in need of paint. I pull out Oma's map. Look again at the church, at the stores.

"Those stores are these stores, aren't they?" I say, showing my mother the map.

"Looks like it. Why?"

"Those were all the Jewish stores. *Der Klein-Jud, Der Schwartz-Jud, Der Weiss-Jud* where Oma always bought her head kerchiefs."

We sit in silence. My mother stirs the remains of her coffee absently. Despite the oppressive heat, she shivers.

"Come, let's get out of here."

IN THE LENGTHENING SHADOWS of evening, we leave Hungary. By the time we reach our hotel room, I am giddy with the heat, overloaded by all we have seen. We sit together on the bed, comparing bust lines and toe flexibility, feeling silly and elated. My mother takes my hand and shakes it, and we congratulate ourselves on a long, exhilarating day.

THE NEXT MORNING, after touring the medieval fortress at Güssing, we are driving along the hilly, twisting Austrian roads between it and the border, searching for Langzeil, the village where Oma and her children weathered the last weeks of war. We are learning that the locals consider road signs superfluous.

"No, go that way!" my mother shouts just after we pass through another crooked, unmarked intersection. For what feels like the hundredth time, I search for a place to turn around. The road she has chosen leads us consistently upwards, growing ever narrower as it climbs.

My mother looks down into the valley and shakes her head. "I'm telling you, if we go over the edge, that's it, we're dead. They'll never find us."

I groan. At every turn in these hills she sucks air sharply between clenched teeth and grips the door. This is becoming increasingly difficult to ignore.

When the road before us dwindles to a cow path, I turn the car around and stop. The land surrounding us is deeply rolling, with hills high enough to make my ears pop. Clusters of red-roofed houses are tucked into the folds of these hills like enchanted hamlets in a Tolkien novel. The gentle slopes are seeded with grapes or corn or brilliant sunflowers. We sit in silence at the top of this little world. It is beautiful.

Halfway back into the valley, we meet another car, hurtling toward us with impossible speed.

"Laura!" my mother gasps, grabbing at my arm. I swerve as far to the edge of the single lane as possible. The other driver nonchalantly does the same and we don't even touch mirrors. As soon as I can, I pull over.

"Look, do you want to drive?" I say to her.

My mother looks at me in surprise.

"Why? I couldn't. You're doing a fantastic job."

In the valley we stop at a *Gasthaus* for directions. Four sunburned men are sitting at a table outside, drinking beer. My mother jumps out with the map to ask where we are. As I walk over to join her, the men look me over.

"Can we come too?" one asks. The others grin.

Back in the car, my mother laughs for a long time.

"See," she says, "you have nothing to worry about."

By a complete fluke we find ourselves in Langzeil. As the stork flies, we must be directly behind Jakobshof.

My mother looks out over the densely wooded hills into Hungary. "Such a long, long way to walk."

I, too, am trying to imagine Oma fleeing over those hills, with Rudi on her back and my mother in her arms. I scan the forest for clearings where the trenches and artillery would have been. A hunter's rifle sounds somewhere in the trees and I flinch.

We ask a woman with a gentle German shepherd if there are paths into the forest.

"Oh, no," she replies.

"Why not?"

"*Ha*, until ten years ago, if you'd gone into those woods, you'd have been shot." I think of the church, of how easily we sauntered across a line that had been patrolled by soldiers ordered to shoot on sight.

We are standing in an empty field on the crest of a hill from which we can see into the valleys on both sides of the border. A gentle wind sweeps through the brilliant sea of meadow flowers that reach our knees, and cow bells clink faintly from deep in the valleys. My mother opens her arms wide and spins around like Maria in *The Sound of Music*.

"This, this spot, is where I'll build my retirement home," she says. I cannot tell if she is serious.

I RETURN TO THE HOTEL from an evening visit to the stables down the road elated. It has felt so good to be on familiar ground, talking horse-talk and being free to represent myself. I have been trying all week to break my mother of the habit of speaking for me. When we are together like this, I am the daughter, she is the adult. People address the adult.

As I chatter animatedly about the Hanoverians and Haflingers, about the interesting woman I met who races two-horse marathon wagons, about the rooms she rents at a fraction of the price we are paying at the hotel, my mother's face darkens.

"What?" I ask.

"I take you all the way to Europe when I could have left you in a barn at home and you'd have been just as happy."

I pull my shoes off and sit on the bed. Where did that come from? I try to explain that I am no longer thirteen and obsessed with horses, that of course I am enjoying myself and am finding this trip incredibly important. She goes to bed and turns her body to the wall.

I am mystified. "Can't you at least tell me what's wrong?"

Silence.

"Look, don't ruin this trip without at least explaining what the problem is!"

"I do all this for you and still you can't appreciate it," she says. "You always make me feel so guilty."

My mind races through the past days, registering every time I turned the car around unnecessarily, waited for her endless beauty routines, went along with her plans. "I, um, thought we were on this adventure together."

Silence.

"Hello? Talk to me!"

From the open window comes the buzz of mosquitoes. I shut it and turn out the lights.

In the morning, she is distant. Makes snide comments about how long *I'm* taking to get ready. I try to stay calm and hope her mood will pass after she has her coffee. It doesn't.

When we are in the car again, I decide to lose it. To quite consciously, deliberately, lose it.

"Look, just what is your problem?" I say.

"You are," she says peevishly, looking out the window.

I take a deep breath. "You make me so angry!" I shout as we hurtle past orchards and pumpkin fields. "Why won't you ever just talk it out? You decide to be mad and then act like a two-year-old who can't explain why. I hate it," I scream, "I fucking hate it!" Tears stream down my face and I welcome their saltiness. My mother has shifted against the door, stunned. No one ever yells back at her, I realize, pleased.

My mother rallies. "Why do you have to analyse everything all the time?"

"I'm not analysing, I just want to talk about it, talk it out."

"Why can't you just live, just get on with living, like normal people do?"

"You're calling yourself normal?"

Suddenly she has had enough. Starts commenting on the weather, on the villages we are passing through, but I'm not finished yet. For once I am going to decide when the argument is over.

Suddenly a light goes on. "It's Oma, isn't it?" I say.

She looks at me blankly.

"It's Oma who makes you feel guilty, not me. She's been telling you all these years that you haven't raised me well, that you should have been around more for me and all that. Surely you can see that she's wrong. That you're both wrong."

"Maybe," she says quietly.

The road we are on is climbing again. I shift down into second gear and feel the remainder of the tension dissolve into the engine's whine.

OMA'S FATHER CAME FROM DEUTSCH MINIHOF, Oma says, south of Heiligenkreutz. It is not on our map, and my mother tosses the useless sheet into the back seat. A grinning farmer has told us, *Immer groad aus*—just keep going straight. Seconds later the road forks. Now we are comfortably lost again in these lush green hills. Miraculously, at the next intersection is a sign. It points right, to a place called Maria Bild. Somehow this sounds familiar, so I turn. For once my mother stays silent.

The road winds upward around hairpin turns that make even my knuckles whiten on the wheel. Finally the forest clears to reveal a tiny church and some houses perched on the hilltop.

The building we park in front of is the fire hall, and a young man is setting up long tables and a sound system for a celebration. Volunteer fire brigades are always having such drinking *Fests*.

We make our way toward the church. The sign I stop to read explains that this hill, this church, is an ancient place of pilgrimage for people from all over. The sign urges everyone who comes to this place to find the space to contemplate, and to be open to whatever we might find.

"Laura, come look at this," my mother calls. I join her in front of a stone war memorial, bright flowers planted at its base. There are names chiselled from both World Wars. Familiar names like Binder and Schrei.

My mother draws her eyebrows together. "Do you think…"

I see her mouthing the words, but they are completely absorbed into the sudden booming of the stereo speakers. Bad English pop music is cranked up so unbearably loud that I can't think. Thunder rumbles in the distance, promising relief from the heat. The clouds are purple-black in the diminishing sunlight.

We take refuge from the music in the little church. Our presence startles a sparrow, which renews its attempts to find a way out. All sound is hushed behind the thick stone walls and the light trickling through the stained glass is filtered and dim. My mother joins me in the back pew.

"So, who are they?" she asks, motioning with her head in the direction of the memorial.

"Well, one fits for sure," I say. "Joseph Schrei. That's your grandfather's name, right?"

"Yes. I used to laugh, because Oma's parents were Joseph and Maria."

"And Joseph died in 1918. That's the date on the stone."

My mother looks at me.

"So we've found them," she whispers, her words echoing faintly in the empty church.

IT IS RAINING ON THE HILL above Mogersdorf. We have happened upon another war memorial, fashioned from the base of a ruined chapel. Beside it a massive cross marks the hill, which saw fierce fighting in both World Wars. We huddle beneath our umbrellas and read plaques informing us that this hill holds much older significance: it marks a major fourteenth-century defeat of the invading Turks by a joint force of French, Austrian and Hungarian troops. There is an illustration of the battle zone.

"Look, that's the Raba," my mother says, pointing to a blue, wavy line. St. Gotthard is also evident on these fourteenth century battle plans.

I trace the line of the river flowing through Oma's fields and wonder aloud if this place has ever been anything but a borderland.

WE STOP FOR COFFEE in the *Gasthaus* on the hill. I can't but overhear the people behind us, who are speaking just like Oma. We turn around and ask them for further directions to Deutsch Minihof. As it turns out they are Binders too. Julius Binder and his wife Mari from Mogersdorf.

When Julius sees my astonished expression he laughs. "Every village around here has its Binders. Schreis there are a lot of, too."

We talk further, and discover that Mari's grandmother went to Allentown, Pennsylvania around the turn of the century.

"I bet she knew my great-grandmother," I exclaim. And Mari's own mother, who is still alive, worked in a factory in St. Gotthard in the years before the war. Suddenly we are exchanging addresses, to see if Oma knows Mari's mother.

When my mother explains that our family had to leave after the war, Julius nods knowingly.

"*Ja,* lots of people left after the war. Over 250,000 Burgenländer left. No work. A steamer line even opened a special office in Graz."

"But our people didn't want to go," my mother explains again. "They were forced. They were deported."

"They were? *Mein Gott,*" Mari murmurs, shaken.

Julius shifts in his chair. "There was so much propaganda, and then the communists came and they told us…" His voice trails off.

Mari looks down into her hands. "I had no idea."

Back in the car I sit shaking my head. "Can you believe it? Practically neighbours and no one knows. Twelve kilometres between them and there might as well have been an ocean."

"*Ha, es woar Krieg,*" says my mother, choosing Oma's words: it was war.

I can only shake my head again.

It is getting dark. The cross on the hill is glowing, surreal with reflected light from the low clouds. Deutsch Minihof will have to wait for morning.

THE HOTEL ROOM IN HEILIGENKREUTZ is cool for once. A fine mist is blowing in through the open window, dampening our pillows. My shoes still on, I stretch out on the bed and close my eyes. My mother is downstairs calling Alexander's sister Christine, arranging for us to meet tomorrow night when we are back in Munich.

"Christine says hallo," my mother informs me when she returns. "She'll meet us at the *Hauptbahnhof.*"

I smile, smelling the nutty, dark pumpkin oil we have purchased for her from a farmer.

My mother changes into her nightdress and goes to the sink to wash.

"You know, Alexander was the problem child, didn't speak to his parents for a whole year," she says.

I blink. "Really?"

"When he was living with that woman in Berlin and she went with him for a visit, his parents wouldn't let them sleep together, so he didn't talk to them for a year. Said it was hypocritical of them.

"That was Alexander," she says, smiling into the sink. "Everything about him was extreme."

I sit up on the bed, my head spinning. Here we are, my mother and I, talking about Alexander as though that were the most natural thing in the world.

"Tell me how you two met."

"I knew him from the hotel in Mainz, you know that," she mumbles into a towel.

"Tell me again?" I ask hesitantly.

"Well, he was the front desk manager at the Hilton in Mainz. That's where we stayed when we flew to Frankfurt, and I flew there a lot in those days. One day he took me for coffee. We had a nice time, but I thought, no chance. He lived in Germany, for starters. He was five years younger. And at first I thought he was gay, being so attractive and single. A lot of our friends were. In our business, you never know.

"And so the months went by, and there would be little notes waiting for me at the desk, friendly notes. I was so blind that I didn't know who they were from. Finally my friend Ricki took me aside and said, 'Look, he seems like a terrific guy, go for it.'

"So then we went out for dinner, and things went from there. We dated for two years, long distance. I tried to get Frankfurt layovers as often as possible. He was really keen on moving abroad. And he loved children. Couldn't wait to meet you."

"I guess I really hampered your dating efforts," I say.

"No," my mother replies, "no, I didn't look at it like that. It was simple. If he wasn't interested in you, I wasn't interested in him." She takes a cotton ball full of makeup remover and presses it against her eye.

"Yes, he was so excited about moving to Canada," she continues. "But we didn't really think it through well enough, work-wise. In Germany you do a long apprenticeship to work in the hotel industry. They didn't respect his training over here at all. He left all his responsibility and respect behind the desk at the Hilton in Mainz. He didn't realize how hard that would be."

"Is that what you two used to fight about?" I ask.

My mother's eyes focus on my reflection in the mirror. Her gaze breaks and she tucks a loose strand of hair behind her ear. "I think he would have been happier in the end if he'd stayed in Germany."

"What do you mean?" I ask her. "You don't think he would have stayed healthy, do you?"

She shrugs. "You never know. Maybe. It's hard to know when he got sick, when he started to change…"

She closes her eyes and spreads moisturizing cream across her face in long, smooth strokes. I feel her moving away.

"Mom, do you think love between two people is ever even?"

She turns to me. "I don't know that it can be. We each love so differently."

I talk for a while about my boyfriend, and she sits down beside me, absorbed. I am savouring this intimacy. "Do you think it's possible to creep into love?"

"Oh absolutely. With your dad for instance, it took a while before I knew."

"It did? I imagined it to be one of those passionate love-at-first-sight moments of total connection…"

She is laughing. "Oh no. It was up and down, such a drama."

I think for a moment. "Does that mean I can never be sure?"

"Certainty is highly overrated in this world, my *Schnukele*," she replies, her voice suddenly tired.

"I guess we're more alike than I'd thought," I muse.

"No, I don't think so," she says, hugging me.

"Thanks," I say. "Thanks for the advice."

"Glad I can be of help." I can hear gratitude in her voice.

DEUTSCH MINIHOF IS SMALLER than Jakobshof. In the early morning rain, there is no one about for us to ask if any Schreis still live here. But once again we find a war memorial. And again he is there. Joseph Schrei, 1918. This time there can be no doubt.

"Oma says this is his home village, and that's his name," I say. "It has to be him."

My mother looks around at the sleeping houses, the profusion of flowers everywhere, vibrant in the rain. "So this is where it all began."

I think of Jakobshof and the church in the woods. Of Unterradling, St. Gotthard and Langzeil, of the whole region we have explored. "Yes," I say, "some of it, at least."

We stand together in silence. Here we are for the first time in a place where people speak our language. Where every town has its Schreis and Binders. Where there is history, our history, in every village square, in every church, on every road my Oma walked. And it is a beautiful spot, this place where we come from. This is what we have found.

I take pictures of the memorial for Oma, and we look around once more. From a nearby house comes the unmistakable smell of bread baking in a *Holzofen*. I grab my mother's hand impulsively and swing it. Our umbrellas touch and bob together as we walk down the glistening street.

Acknowledgements

MY THANKS TO Margaret Mapstone, Rhonda Shirreff, and Gillian Siddall for early encouragement, and to Janice Kulyk Keefer for helping me lay the groundwork.

For his meticulous and perceptive editing and for teaching me how to write, I'm indebted to Greg Hollingshead.

Thank you to the creative writing workshop and all those who read early drafts of this work: Jacqueline Baker, Gordon and Betty Bray, Hermann and Erne Kozel, Chris Magwood, Heather McClinchy, Greg and Linda Taylor.

A huge thank you to Ben Polley and Tracy Rockett for being great cheerleaders, and to Archana Rampure and Heather Guezen for much sage advice.

Thanks to everyone at Shoreline Press and to Hugh Banfill for building the family tree; to Kathe Gray and Scott Mooney for their contributions to the design of this book; to Trina Koster for the fab author photo; to Anne Hayter for proofreading; to John Denison, Esther Vincent, Natale Ghent, Ajay Heble, and Charlene Diehl for their invaluable advice and help in the latter stages of this project; to poet Kristiane Allert-Wybranietz for allowing me to use a passage of her verse as the epigraph for this book.

I owe everything to Oma for being a storyteller, and also to Frank for his contributions. Thank you to the rest of my family for humouring the storytellers among us.

A special thank you to my wonderful mother for her incredible support in all areas of my life. I sincerely hope that she enjoys this book more than she thinks she will.

And for holding us all together, warm thanks to Fred Keist.

TRINA KOSTER

LAURA ELISE TAYLOR has studied creative writing with Janice Kulyk Keefer and Greg Hollingshead, and holds an M.A. from the University of Alberta. Born in Port Credit, Ontario, she works as a freelance writer and documentary photographer in Guelph, Ontario. She is the coauthor and main photographer of a popular science book on cottage culture, forthcoming from Boston Mills Press in 2006. When not writing or shooting you will find her on a canoe trip, salsa dancing, or, if she's lucky, on the road less travelled.